INVESTING MONEY

NEW YORK STOCK EXCHANGE

The main trading floor of the New York Stock Exchange.

INVESTING MONEY

THE FACTS ABOUT STOCKS AND BONDS

RUTH BRINDZE

Illustrated with photographs
and line drawings

HARCOURT, BRACE & WORLD, INC., NEW YORK

by the same author

THE RISE AND FALL OF THE SEAS
The Story of the Tides

Copyright © 1968 by Ruth Brindze

FM

FIRST EDITION

Library of Congress Catalog Card Number: 68–28801

PRINTED IN THE UNITED STATES OF AMERICA

CONTENTS

1
MILLIONS OF PARTNERS

More than twenty million people own shares in the business corporations that make the products and provide the services all of us use. Your parents or your friend's parents may be stockholders in the American Telephone and Telegraph Company, the General Electric Company, the General Motors Corporation, the Radio Corporation of America, or in one or more of thousands of other businesses. People with money to invest have a wide choice of companies in which they can purchase a part interest.

Most shareholders never see their company's factories, laboratories, or offices; they do not take part in the operation of the business. But as owners of a company's common stock (the kind of stock the average investor buys), they have a say in what is done. They elect a board of directors to act as their representatives, and on some matters they vote directly. Ordinarily, stockholders are entitled to cast one vote for each share they own; the more shares a person owns in a company, the greater is his power to control.

Companies sell shares to obtain capital to start a business or to expand it. New corporations are usually owned by a small group of stockholders who are acquainted with each other. After Alexander Graham Bell invented the telephone and went into business, shares in the Bell Telephone Company were divided among four men, Bell, his assistant, and two others who had supplied the inventor with money for his experiments.

Bell's small company became the vast organization named the American Telephone and Telegraph Company. Shares in it are owned by more than three million men, women, and children* living throughout the United States and in other parts of the world.

Comparatively recently, the American Telephone and Telegraph Company needed more than a billion dollars for an expansion program. The company obtained the money from its stockholders. With their approval the company issued additional shares that the stockholders had the right to buy at a very favorable price. They paid their company nearly $1,250,000,000 for the stock. Only because the public provides the capital are privately owned big businesses possible.

---

* Although the law prohibits the buying of securities by anyone under the age of twenty-one, over a million and a quarter boys and girls own stock bought in their names by parents and other adults.

In addition to selling the public shares, corporations also borrow money from the public. They do this by selling bonds. The federal government, states, cities, and innumerable official agencies also obtain funds from the sale of bonds.

There are times when it is more advantageous for a company to borrow than to sell shares. And some people prefer to lend rather than to buy shares in a business. A person who buys a bond knows how much interest he can count on receiving each year since the rate is fixed, as is the date when the payment of his loan is due. Also, bondholders have the first claim on a company's earnings and assets. Bondholders must be paid before stockholders of a company get anything.

Payments to holders of a company's common stock are based on profits. How much they receive depends on what their company earns. If a company is successful, its stockholders may receive a higher return on their investment than the company's bondholders. In addition, shares in a successful company increase in value. Owners may be able to sell their shares for many times the price they paid. This is not generally true of bonds. No matter how well a company does, there is usually no big jump in the value of its bonds, and when they become due, they are worth no more than the amount printed on them.

Of course, not all companies succeed. Risk is present in any business operation, small or large. However, when buying stocks or bonds, just as when making other investments, there are ways of determining the extent of the risk.

If an individual opens a business of his own and it does badly, the owner not only loses the money he invested in the venture, but he is also responsible for all the debts incurred by the business. The situation is the same if a group of people form a partnership to operate, say, a candy store, and fail to attract enough customers to make the business pay. Each of the partners is personally liable for the debts of the business.

Shareholders in a corporation are in a different position. Although each owns a part of the corporation, he is not generally liable for its debts. As a practical matter, even if a corporation becomes bankrupt, the most its stockholders can lose is the amount they paid for their shares. This limited liability is the distinguishing feature of business corporations. The limited liability corporation is a legal invention that has made possible our large-scale businesses. Few people would buy stock if by doing so they became liable for the corporation's debts.

Similarly, investing in large corporations or lending money to them would not be as popular as it is if it were not for the ease with which stocks and bonds can be bought and sold. A man who wishes to sell his own small business must wait until he finds a buyer. The sale or purchase of the securities (stocks and bonds) of large companies can be completed within minutes. There is a highly organized marketing system for handling the transactions.

The New York Stock Exchange is the oldest and most important stock market in the United States. An average day's business in 1967 involved the trading of close to 10 million shares of stock with a market value of more than 400 million dollars. An exchange does not own the securities sold in its trading rooms, nor does it set prices. Brokers representing buyers and sellers bargain to get the best prices for their customers. Like all other stock markets, the New York Stock Exchange is a brokers' organization. Only brokers who are members of an exchange may use its facilities to carry out their customers' orders to buy or to sell.

Trading at exchanges is limited to the stocks and bonds of companies that meet the exchange's eligibility rules and are listed by it. The New York Stock Exchange requires applicants to have annual earnings of at least $2,000,000 (before the payment of taxes) and a minimum of 2,000 shareholders. Only the largest companies can meet these requirements.

Some companies do not apply for listing to any organized market. Their stocks and bonds are bought and sold in what is known as the over-the-counter market. Don't be confused by the name; most over-the-counter trading is done by telephone.

Market prices—what securities are bought or sold for —continually change. For example, at 10 A.M. a sale is made of 100 shares in Good Prospects' Company at $45 per share. A half hour later another seller asks, and gets, $45.25 per share for his 100 shares in Good Prospects' Company. Price depends on what a buyer is willing to pay, and a seller to take, at the time a deal is made.

A company does not make a cent when the market price of its shares rises. And a company loses nothing if the market price of its shares falls. Companies get their financing from the first sale of their stocks and bonds. After the first sale, whoever owns the securities gains or loses as a result of changes in their market price.

Because market prices fluctuate, up-to-the-minute price information is important to buyers and sellers. In 1867 the New York Stock Exchange began to send reports of transactions at the Exchange to brokers' offices by means of a telegraphic printing device called a "ticker." The Exchange's present high-speed ticker system is capable of transmitting 900 letters and figures a minute, which is about as fast as a person can read. The "900" ticker was designed to keep up with the market news even on days when trading is unusually heavy. In addition to the reports sent directly from stock markets, financial news is broadcast by radio and television and is published in newspapers.

Market prices indicate what people think of a company's prospects. If many people think they are good and bid for the company's stock, its price goes up. If many people think a company's prospects are only so-so and more people want to sell than to buy, the price of the stock falls.

But you can't tell from market price alone whether shares in a company are a good investment or a poor one. You need the facts about a company's financial situation. In former days little such information was made public. But in the early 1930's, during Franklin D. Roosevelt's first term as President, laws were enacted requiring large publicly owned companies to disclose the state of their business. This is only one of the provisions of the "truth in securities" laws. They have made fundamental changes in the operation of the security business, and all these changes benefit the public.

Wall Street in New York City is the financial center of the United States. The New York Stock Exchange began its operations on Wall Street in 1792. Today the Exchange's building on narrow Wall Street is surrounded by skyscrapers in which banks and brokerage firms have their main offices. Wall Street is one of the sights to see in New York, and a visit to the New York Stock Exchange is the high point of a tour of the financial district.

2

THE NEW YORK
STOCK EXCHANGE
IN ACTION

When you first look down at the main trading floor of the New York Stock Exchange from the visitors' gallery, everything seems hectic. The floor, about two-thirds the size of a football field, is crowded with men, some standing in groups, others walking rapidly in various directions. Scraps of paper litter the floor.

The trading room is of great height. From floor to ceiling it measures seventy-nine feet, which is about as high as a six-story office building. On the side of the room facing Wall Street, daylight streams in through seven tall windows. On two other walls there are large "callboards" on which numbers flash on and off, the changes being accompanied by a clack. Each member of the Exchange is assigned a number, which is flashed simultaneously on both boards when one of his clerks wishes to communicate with him. Clerks, working in enclosures bordering the trading floor, receive orders by telephone and teletype from their firm's offices. Members who do the trading move from one part of the room to another but can always be reached because, no matter where they are, they keep an eye on one of the call-boards.

The centers of activity are twelve horseshoe-shaped counters. These are the trading posts. Six more are in an adjoining room known as the "garage." The stock of about eighty companies is traded at each post. Trading takes place around the outside of the posts. There is a separate room where bonds are bought and sold.

Only members, their assistants, and employees of the Exchange are permitted on the trading floor. Each wears a badge or a jacket of a color that indicates his category. Pages wear gray jackets; the Exchange's reporters who record stock transactions wear black jackets. All members wear oval-shaped white badges on or near the left lapel of their jackets. Their telephone clerks' badges are oblong and have a picture of the wearer printed on a yellowish background.

After a few moments of watching—from the visitors' gallery—the general movement on the main trading floor, you begin to notice individuals. One man wearing a member's badge is walking rapidly toward the trading post nearest your position on the gallery. The post, Number 1, is where the stock of United Air Lines is traded.

The man heading for post Number 1 has just been given an order to buy 100 shares of United Air Lines' stock. As he approaches the group gathered at the position where the stock is traded, he glances at the indicator on the post that shows the price at which the stock was last sold. The next sale may be made at the same price or for a lower or a higher price.

A standardized procedure is used for trading. If you could listen in to what is said after your man joins the group, you would hear something like the following. Your man asks, "How's United?" He does not indicate whether he wants to buy or to sell.

"Seventy-six and one half, seventy-six and three quarters," someone in the group answers. This verbal shorthand means that the highest bid is $76.50 a share, and the lowest offer to sell is $76.75.

Your man remains silent for a few seconds. Sometimes a seller lowers his price, or another seller may come along and be willing to accept less than the price previously named. If the selling price remains firm, a broker who wants to buy does some bargaining. In the transaction used here as an illustration, he might make an offer of 76 and ⅝. This is one-eighth of a dollar more per share than the amount previously bid, and one-eighth of a dollar less than any seller has said he would accept. In buying or selling stock, one-eighth is the smallest price differential used.

In our illustration a broker with an order to sell decides that he cannot get more than the 76 and ⅝ ($76.625) that has been bid, and he says, "Sold." This two-way public auction system with buyers and sellers competing publicly is unique to trading at stock exchanges.

After a price is agreed upon, the two brokers make brief notations about the transaction. No written agreement is exchanged. The brokers report the transaction to their clerks, who notify their firms. The firms, in turn, notify the customers that their orders have been carried out. Frequently, orders are filled within minutes after they are given.

Immediately after a transaction is concluded, an official record is made of it by the Exchange's reporter at the trading post. He draws a few lines through coded boxes on a specially designed IBM card and slips it into an electronic scanning instrument. The scanner relays the data on the card to the Exchange's computer center, where it is stored in memory drums and at the same time transmitted by wire to brokers' offices throughout the country and to many overseas. At the end of the day, the Exchange's bookkeeping department tallies up members' accounts to show what they have sold and bought.

About half of the 1,366 members of the Exchange are *commission house brokers.* They are partners or officers of brokerage firms that handle the purchase and sale of securities for the public. Such firms are known as commission houses because they charge a commission for their services. A commission house broker executes on the floor of the Exchange the orders his firm receives from its customers. Many firms are represented at the Exchange by more than one broker.

If all its brokers are busy when a firm's clerk at the Exchange receives an order, he may give it to a *floor broker* to fill. Men in this category act as substitutes for commission house brokers and are paid by their firms. In former days floor brokers received $2 for handling an order; their fees are higher now, but the popular name for floor brokers still is "$2 brokers."

At the New York Stock Exchange, the standard unit of trading for most stock is 100 shares. One hundred shares, or multiples of 100, is known as a round lot. Any number of shares from 1 to 99 is known as an odd lot. Buy and sell orders for odd lots are not handled in the same way as for round lots. Commission house brokers give their odd-lot orders to Exchange members who function as *odd-lot dealers.*

An odd-lot dealer maintains a supply of securities. He can't sell or buy for any price he wishes. His price is determined by the next round-lot transaction in the stock. As an illustration, an odd-lot dealer given an order for 25 shares in Typical Company would wait until a round-lot sale is made of the stock. Assume the selling price is $40 a share. The odd-lot dealer thereupon sells his 25 shares at $40 each to which is added the charge for his services. The New York Stock Exchange's schedule provides for a charge of 12½ cents a share on stock priced at less than $55 and 25 cents a share for stock selling at $55 or more. To the odd-lot dealer's fee the investor's brokerage firm adds its commission. The commission rate is lower than that for round-lot purchases and sales, which helps to equalize the charges on odd-lot and round-lot transactions.

About thirty of the New York Stock Exchange's members trade only for themselves. They are known as *regis-*

Like most stock certificates, Greyhound's is a fraction over twelve by eight inches. In this size every word is legible.

tered traders. There are many restrictions on their buying and selling. At least 75 percent of all their transactions must have a stabilizing effect on market prices. To comply with this requirement, registered traders must do most of their buying when stock prices are falling and most of their selling when stock prices are rising. By doing this, they counterbalance downswings and upswings. Registered traders must give the Exchange a daily record of their trading. Despite the restrictions on their trading, men who are expert in judging stock values make money as registered traders.

About 360 members of the New York Stock Exchange

are *specialists*. They are appointed to act in this capacity by the Exchange. When a company's stock is accepted for listing, members who function as specialists apply to the Exchange to have the stock assigned to them. Assignments are made on the basis of the applicant's performance record and his ability to meet the financial requirements set by the Exchange.

Specialists have two big jobs. First, they are expected to maintain a fair and orderly market for the stocks assigned to them, and second, they must effectively execute orders entrusted to them by other Exchange members.

A specialist may be appointed "to make a market" for the stock of a dozen or more companies. The trading post at which a stock is bought and sold depends on the specialist to whom it is assigned. All stock handled by the same specialist is traded at the same post. Unlike commission house brokers, who move from one trading post to another to fill their orders, a specialist remains at his post.

To perform his function, a specialist must trade in the stocks assigned to him, buying or selling them in order to maintain an orderly market. For example, if the public's highest bid and lowest asking price are so far apart that trading is at a standstill, the specialist goes into action. Either he sells from his own supply at a lower price than any other seller has named, or he buys for his own account at a higher price than any other buyer has bid. Such a purchase or sale narrows the spread between the public's bid and asking prices and encourages the resumption of trading. A specialist requires a considerable amount of money on which he can draw to buy stock and to maintain a supply of it.

Specialists are expected to prevent rapid fluctuations of the market prices of the stocks they service. The Exchange states that: "The specialist is not expected to prevent a stock from declining nor is he expected to keep it from going up. He is expected to try to keep rises and declines fair and orderly, insofar as is reasonably practicable under the circumstances."

Performing this duty is both difficult and dramatic when something happens that results in a rush of buying or selling by the public. A good illustration is the situation that the specialist in Lockheed Aircraft Corporation faced in 1964 after President Johnson announced that the aircraft company was to develop a supersonic plane for the government. Building the new planes would vastly increase Lockheed's business, and the public was eager to buy stock in the company.

The President's announcement was made on Saturday, February 29. Before the Exchange opened on the following Monday, orders to buy 30,000 shares of Lockheed stock had been received by commission house brokers. It is standard procedure to turn over orders received prior to the opening of the Exchange to the specialist in the stock.

Specialists also fill limit orders, so called because the customer specifies, or limits, the price at which he will buy or sell. Commission house brokers cannot wait at a post until the specified price is reached, but specialists always remain at their posts and can carry out limit orders. Every specialist has a book in which he records the orders given to him and the exact time of their receipt. If there is more than one order to buy or to sell at the same price, the first one received is filled first. Then, if possible, the second order is carried out, and so on down the list.

Before the supersonic plane was announced, the specialist in Lockheed had, in his book, orders to sell about 17,000 shares, or a little more than half as many as the buy orders. Unless supply and demand were brought into better balance, the price of Lockheed stock would soar. To increase the supply of the stock, the specialist decided to sell, for his own account, 9,600 shares of Lockheed. He arranged with registered traders to sell 3,200 additional shares. With these, the shares the specialist had for sale almost equaled his buy orders.

It was obvious to the Exchange authorities, to brokers, and to the public that there would be a price rise in Lockheed stock when trading started. However, because the specialist had a supply of the stock, he was in a position to prevent its price from skyrocketing. The specialist could match his buy and sell orders at a price that was $2.75 more per share than the last price paid on Friday. Because the price change was greater than normal—market prices usually change by a fraction of a dollar—the specialist was required to consult the Exchange authorities and obtain their approval of his price.

Trading begins at the New York Stock Exchange with the clanging of a bell at ten o'clock in the morning. Within thirty-three minutes after the bell was sounded, the Lockheed specialist had filled his buy orders. During the day, 111,700 shares in Lockheed were traded. The specialist bought for his own account when there were fewer buyers than sellers, and sold from his supply when there were more buyers than sellers. The result was that prices were kept under control. During the day no transaction varied in price from the preceding one by more than 25¢ a share.

Most visitors to the New York Stock Exchange see only the main trading floor and neither the "garage" nor the bond trading room. The bond room is a quiet place compared with the main trading floor. A relatively small percentage of the business done at the Exchange is in bonds.

Although only large companies can meet the New York Stock Exchange's requirements for listing, any that qualify are accepted. The policy as to membership in the Exchange is different. Membership is limited to a fixed number. The only way of obtaining a membership is to wait until one is offered for sale. As much as $445,000 has been paid in recent years for a membership or a "seat" as it is usually called. The term is a leftover from the days when members conducted their trading while seated. In addition to the amount paid for a membership, there is an initiation fee of $7,500. Annual dues are $1,500. The ability to pay the price does not assure a candidate that he will be accepted. Approval by the Exchange is required.

Rules and policies are set by the Exchange's Board of Governors, a group of thirty-three men, who are either members of the Exchange or affiliated members—that is, partners in firms or holders of voting stock in member corporations. Two-thirds of the Governors are affiliated members. The Exchange does not aim at making a profit. Most of its more than $40,000,000 annual income, derived from charges to members and listed companies, is spent for operating expenses.

Of the other organized stock markets in the United States, the American Stock Exchange, also located in New York City, is second in importance to the "Big Board." Basically the operation of the American Exchange and of the smaller regional exchanges is similar to that of the New York Stock Exchange. Many brokerage firms are represented by partners or officers at the New York Stock Exchange, the American Stock Exchange, and at one or more regional stock exchanges.

Although companies can be listed on only one of the two New York stock markets, they may, in addition, be listed by any number of regional exchanges. Regional exchanges are primarily markets for the stock of local companies, but at times they handle heavy trading in the stock of national companies.

After the cease-fire in the 1967 war between the United Arab Republic and Israel, many people believed that stock prices would rise and wished to buy as soon as possible. News of the cease-fire came too late for orders to be filled before the New York exchanges closed at 3:30 P.M. The Pacific Stock Exchange, which has branches in Los Angeles and San Francisco, is in the Pacific time zone and remains open three hours after the New York markets have closed. Orders for stock listed on the New York and Pacific Coast exchanges were telephoned to

California from the East Coast and from as far away as London and Paris. The phone orders accounted for one-third of the 361,000 shares of stock traded at the Pacific Stock Exchange during the day.

Formerly, stock markets gave relatively little attention to the protection of the public. Now stock exchanges closely regulate trading and the conduct of their members. And the entire securities business is policed by the government through the Securities and Exchange Commission.

3

THE TRUTH IN SECURITIES LAWS

The Securities Act of 1933, the first of the "truth in securities" laws, marked the beginning of a new era for investors. In his message to Congress urging the enactment of the legislation, President Franklin D. Roosevelt said that the bill he was recommending added "to the ancient rule of *caveat emptor* (Latin for 'let the buyer beware') the further doctrine, let the seller also beware. It puts the burden of telling the whole truth on the seller." The President was referring to companies whose stocks and bonds are sold to the public.

The 1933 act requires companies offering new issues of stocks or bonds to supply sufficient information so that prospective buyers can judge the merit of the securities. And it prohibits misrepresentation, deceit, and other fraudulent practices in the sale of securities.

The Securities Exchange Act of 1934 increased federal regulation of the security business. All securities traded at stock markets and the markets themselves were brought under control. To administer the security laws, a special agency, the Securities and Exchange Commission, was created.

The SEC is headed by five commissioners appointed by the President with the consent of the Senate. Commissioners are appointed for a term of five years. Not more than three commissioners may be members of the same political party. Like other administrative agencies, the SEC is empowered to make rules as to what must be done to comply with the laws it enforces. The SEC acts as a court in some cases in which its investigations indicate a possible violation of the security laws. It prosecutes other cases in the regular courts.

Under its rule-making power, the SEC specifies what information companies must supply before they may offer a new issue of stocks or bonds to the public. The official registration form calls for a detailed description of the applicant's business, its financial record for the past few years, information as to the management of the company, a list of the officers and directors, the salaries they are paid, the number of shares they hold in the company, and so on.

If all the facts stated on the application appear to the SEC to be honest and complete, it notifies the company that its new issue of securities has been accepted for registration and may be offered for sale. Weeks or months may elapse before the Commission gives the go-ahead

27

signal. Companies are required to have booklets printed containing a summary of the information supplied to the SEC. A copy of the booklet, called a "prospectus," must be given to everyone to whom a new security is offered. Newspaper advertisements of new securities are limited by law to a mere announcement. They usually state, "This announcement is neither an offer to sell nor a solicitation of offers to buy any of these securities. The offering is made only by the prospectus."

The purpose of requiring the distribution of the prospectus is to provide people considering the purchase of new securities with the data necessary for judging them. The SEC does not have the power to pass on whether a security is a safe investment or a risky one. The evaluation of securities is up to the public. The Commission emphasizes this fact because some people assume that when the SEC grants permission for the sale of securities, it is the equivalent of official approval. The Commission also points out that it does not guarantee the accuracy of the facts in the registration application or in the prospectus. However, the law provides stiff penalties for anyone who makes misleading statements.

Comparatively recently, the SEC stopped the sale of a company's stock because the prospectus did not give the full facts about the project that the company was asking the public to finance. The company had been organized for the purpose of salvaging cargoes of sunken ships. In its prospectus the company stated that it was going to work on a ship that had sunk in the Gulf of Mexico in 1942. Her cargo was described as copper wire and other

NEW ISSUE   March 8, 1968

90,000 Shares

Educational Computer Corporation

Common Stock
(Par Value 10¢ per Share)

Price $7.25 per Share

Copies of the Prospectus may be obtained from the undersigned or selected dealers only in States where these securities may be legally offered.

Smith, Jackson & Company
Incorporated

Pressman, Frohlich & Frost,   Dewey, Johnson & George, Inc.
Incorporated

Herbert Young & Co., Inc.   Mayflower Securities Co., Inc.

Advertisements of new securities are limited by law to a mere announcement.

metal with an estimated value "in excess of two million."

However, when SEC investigators checked the ship's cargo list filed by her captain before he left port, they found no mention of metals. The cargo list included only perishables. The SEC said that the prospectus should

29

have contained a report on the cargo list and, because it had not, prohibited any further offering of the company's stock. It also revoked the license of the broker-dealer who had handled the distribution of the stock. The Commission said that he had not exercised reasonable care as to the accuracy of the material in the prospectus and had made false statements about the value of the securities. In such a situation, the broker, the company, its officers and directors are liable for any loss sustained by people who purchased the securities.

Following the original registration of securities, companies must file periodic reports with the SEC to keep the information up to date. The reports are open for inspection by the public at offices of the SEC or at the stock exchange where the securities are traded. Summaries of the reports are printed in publications for investors. The best known are the ones prepared by Moody's Investors Service and Standard and Poor's Corporation. Copies of these companies' publications are available at many libraries.

In addition to the report filed by a company, each of its officers, directors, and any shareholders who own 10 percent or more of the company's stock must disclose their holdings to the SEC. If they buy more stock or sell any, a revised report must be filed. These reports enable the SEC to keep track of the trading of "insiders."

Prior to the enactment of the truth in securities laws, there was no restriction against insiders using the information available to them, but not to the general public, to make money by trading in their company's stock. An insider is in a position to know, long before the public, of business developments that may result in a rise or fall of the market price of the stock. In former days fortunes were made by people with inside information; today anyone found guilty of using his inside knowledge for his own advantage may be ordered by a court to return his profits to his company.

If stockholders are to vote intelligently on their company's affairs, they must know the facts about the men nominated for the board of directors and about actions that the company proposes to take. The Securities Exchange Act requires that full information be sent to stockholders. The material must be approved by the Commission. Also when a group of stockholders wishes to change the management of a company and to campaign for the votes of other shareowners, the Commission requires the members of the group to disclose how many shares each owns and what they propose to do. Ballot forms must be submitted to the SEC before being sent to shareowners.

Stock markets make their own rules, but they are subject to the Commission's approval. Stock markets must register with the SEC—in other words, be licensed to carry on their business. The Commission has the authority to revoke the registration of an exchange and has done this.

Both the men responsible for the operation of stock markets and the SEC maintain a continual watch to insure that trading is fair. Before the enactment of the security laws, manipulators were free to operate in stock markets. Instead of prices being determined by fair bargaining, gangs of manipulators, known as "pools," rigged prices by tricky maneuvering and dishonest publicity.

A pool picked a company, acquired a large number of shares in it, and then arranged to publicize false reports about the company's prospects. The objective was to start a rush of buying by the public. As a result of the public's bidding for the stock, its price spiraled, and when it reached a point satisfactory to the manipulators, they sold out. Their sale caused an oversupply of the stock in the market, which led to a sharp fall in its price. People who had bought at the artificially inflated prices were trapped. They could sell for only a fraction of what they had paid. The manipulators made profits in millions; the public lost millions. Today the manipulation of stock prices is outlawed; the penalty for a convicted manipulator is a term in prison.

There are lawbreakers in every field, and from time to time attempts to manipulate stock prices still are made. They are usually detected quickly. Computers simplify the detective work. The New York Stock Exchange and other organized stock markets make a daily computerized record of all transactions. Such a record discloses any increased activity in the trading of a company's stock. If there is no apparent reason for the spurt in buying, an investigation is started. The investigators question the brokers who handled the transactions and the buyers of the stock. The SEC either conducts an independent investigation or joins forces with the stock market. While a situation is being investigated, trading in the company's stock may be halted. No one can either buy or sell it.

When a person who has bought or sold securities thinks that he has been cheated, he may ask the SEC for help. The Commission's headquarters are in Washington, D.C., and it has offices in sixteen cities throughout the country. If the investor lives in, or near, a city where the SEC has an office, he may make his complaint in person or by telephone. Or the situation may be described in a letter. Every SEC office has a department that deals with investors' complaints.

Complaints that orders to buy or to sell have not been carried out or that high-pressure selling methods have been used are turned over to the Commission's investigators for thorough checking. Complaints from the public are an important source of leads for the detection of dishonest operations.

In the late 1950's and early 1960's, there was an upsurge of "boiler room" operations. A boiler room is a place used as headquarters by racketeers who deal in worthless or highly risky stock. Boiler-room salesmen solicit business by telephone. They may call anyone whose name is listed in a telephone directory and make up any story that they think will convince their prospective victim to buy. And, unfortunately, some people still buy this way.

Three salesmen in one boiler room that the SEC put out of business described a company whose stock they were peddling as being in the gas business, as a manufacturer of home equipment, and as a prosperous sales organization. One of the salesmen said that the company might earn a quarter of a million dollars during the year. Actually, the company had done no business for six months and then had obtained a contract to sell building lots in Arizona. The contract could be canceled by the owner of the land if he was not satisfied with the number of lots sold. The company was in a dangerous position, yet the boiler-room salesmen promised a spectacular increase in the value of its shares.

Willful misrepresentation of a security is illegal. If the SEC's investigation indicates a violation of the truth in securities laws, the persons involved are notified to appear before the Commission. An SEC hearing is conducted similarly to a court trial. A suspect tells his side of the story and may submit whatever evidence he wishes to prove his innocence. Any member of the public who believes that he has been wronged may testify at the hearing. If the SEC finds a suspect to be guilty, it bars him from the security business.

But putting a dishonest operator out of business does not help people whom he has defrauded. The SEC cannot aid those who have been cheated to get their money back. The only way they can attempt to collect is by suing. Not many do because bringing a court suit is expensive. Wise investors protect themselves against unnecessary losses by following the SEC's ten-point guide:

1. Before buying—think!

THE TRUTH IN SECURITIES LAWS

2. Don't deal with strange securities firms. (Consult your broker, banker, or other experienced person you know and trust.)

3. Beware of securities offered over the telephone by strangers.

4. Don't listen to high-pressure sales talk.

5. Beware of promises of spectacular profits.

6. Be sure you understand the risks of loss.

7. Don't buy on tips and rumors—get all the facts!

8. Tell the salesman to: Put all the information and advice in writing and mail it to you. Save it!

9. If you don't understand all the written information —consult a person who does.

10. Give at least as much consideration to buying securities as you would to buying other valuable property.

4

FINANCIAL HISTORY
OF A BIG BUSINESS

There is no more fascinating example of how a small business develops into a big one owned by thousands of shareholders than the Polaroid Corporation, famous for its cameras that turn out a finished picture in seconds after it has been snapped. Polaroid was organized in 1937 and twenty years later qualified for listing by the New York Stock Exchange.

To tell the company's story from the beginning, we must start back in 1927 when Edward H. Land, president of Polaroid Corporation and inventor of the camera it produces, was a freshman at Harvard College. At the time the blinding glare of automobile headlights was a serious problem. Glare caused countless highway accidents. One night, after watching the dazzling effect of headlights, Land decided that the way to eliminate glare was to equip headlights with polarizing filters.

The fact that the direction in which light waves vibrate can be controlled by polarization was well known. But the scientific principle could not be practically applied because the only polarizing filters available were very expensive. A filter measuring about a square inch cost several hundred dollars.

Land believed that if a low-priced filter could be developed, automobile manufacturers would put them on every car they produced. He envisioned tremendous sales. Land was so intrigued by the idea of inventing a filtering material that he took a leave of absence from college to work on it. After experimenting for a little more than a year, Land developed a material that performed satisfactorily. It looked like grayish cellophane.

The only way to protect one's rights to an invention is by patenting it, and the inventor consulted an expert in patent law. When he filed an application for a patent, the United States Patent Office replied that it was holding other applications for the polarization of headlights and that when passing on them, Land's would be considered. His was the only application based on the use of a novel polarizing material.

Land continued his experiments after he returned to college and produced an improved polarizing material made by embedding crystals made from quinine in thinly rolled plastic sheeting. It was patented in 1933. The year before, Land had quit college to go into business. A quarter of a century later Harvard gave Land an honorary degree of Doctor of Science in recognition of his scientific achievements.

Many businesses are not started as corporations. It is

sometimes simpler for an individual, or for partners, to establish a personally owned company. However, Land's lawyers advised him to incorporate his business.

Its name was Land-Wheelwright Laboratories, Inc., and it had three shareholders, Land, his wife Helen, and George W. Wheelwright III. Land and Wheelwright met at Harvard, where Wheelwright was an instructor in the physics department.

The Lands and Wheelwright financed their company and worked for it. The first important contract for the use of the polarizing material (its trademark name was Polaroid) was made with the Eastman Kodak Company. It contracted to manufacture and sell Polaroid filters for cameras. Another big company, the American Optical Company, contracted to make Polaroid sunglasses.

Land-Wheelwright developed a third market for the polarizing material. It sold schools and colleges discs of the material together with accessory equipment for demonstrating the polarization of light. A new corporation was organized to handle the production and sale of the demonstration outfits.

It is a common practice to keep an enterprise's activities separate. Doing this affords protection. Even though the same people own a group of corporations, each is financially independent of the others. If the demonstration outfit business failed, only the corporation that handled it would be responsible for any debts incurred.

The inventor was unaware that his growing business had attracted the attention of financing specialists. These men scout for promising young companies and arrange for the financing required for their expansion. One of these specialists offered his services to the Lands and Wheelwright. He told them that he would talk to investment bankers about putting money into the Land-Wheelwright organization.

When investment bankers supply funds, they frequently get shares in the business. The arrangement made with the bankers provided for the organization of a new company, named Polaroid Corporation, to which the Lands and Wheelwright would turn over all the stock in their existing companies and the patents they held. Polaroid's charter specified that three classes of stock were to be issued. The first two were preferred stock, the third, common stock.

All preferred stocks get some sort of preferential treatment. Most preferred stock is entitled to a dividend before any dividend can be paid on the common stock of the corporation. The dividend on preferred stock is usually a fixed amount.

The dividend payable on common stock is not fixed in advance; it depends on the earnings of the company. Usually, the directors of corporations meet four times a year to determine what dividend will be paid for each quarterly period.

A preferred stock entitled to a yearly dividend of, say, $5 a year, may be a risky investment if the company's directors have the authority to skip the preferred dividend in any one year and then, the following year, to pay only $5 for that year. To make their preferred stock attractive to investors, most companies issue the type known as cumulative preferred stock. If the company does not earn enough during any dividend period to pay

As filed with the Securities and Exchange Commission November 6, 1958

Registration No. 2-14499

SECURITIES AND EXCHANGE COMMISSION
Washington 25, D. C.

Form S-1

REGISTRATION STATEMENT
Under
THE SECURITIES ACT OF 1933

Polaroid Corporation

(Exact name of registrant as specified in charter)

730 MAIN STREET, CAMBRIDGE 39, MASSACHUSETTS
(Address of principal executive offices)

JULIUS SILVER
Vice President
60 East 42nd Street
New York 17, N. Y.

CARLTON P. FULLER
Vice President, Treasurer
730 Main Street
Cambridge 39, Mass.

(Names and addresses of agents for service)

Approximate date of commencement of proposed sale to the public: As soon as practicable after the Registration Statement becomes effective.

CALCULATION OF REGISTRATION FEE

Title of Each Class of Securities Being Registered	Amount Being Registered	Proposed Maximum Offering Price Per Unit	Proposed Maximum Aggregate Offering Price	Amount of Registration Fee
Common Stock, par value $1 per share (and Subscription Warrants evidencing Rights to purchase such shares)	173,616 shares	$90*	$15,625,440*	$1,562.54

* Estimated solely for the purpose of determining the registration fee.

PRELIMINARY PROSPECTUS DATED NOVEMBER 6, 1958

PROSPECTUS

173,616 Shares

Polaroid Corporation

Common Stock

(Par Value $1 Per Share)

Polaroid Corporation (the "Company") is offering to the holders of its outstanding Common Stock the right, evidenced by transferable Warrants, to subscribe for 173,616 shares of Common Stock at the rate of one share for each 21 shares held of record at the close of business on November 25, 1958, all as more fully set forth under "Subscription Offer" herein.

THESE SECURITIES HAVE NOT BEEN APPROVED OR DISAPPROVED BY THE SECURITIES AND EXCHANGE COMMISSION NOR HAS THE COMMISSION PASSED UPON THE ACCURACY OR ADEQUACY OF THIS PROSPECTUS. ANY REPRESENTATION TO THE CONTRARY IS A CRIMINAL OFFENSE.

SUBSCRIPTION PRICE $ - - — PER SHARE

The Subscription Offer will expire at 3:30 P. M., Eastern Standard Time, on December 9, 1958.

	Subscription Price	Underwriting Discounts and Commissions(1)	Proceeds to Company(1)(2)
Per Share	$_ - -	Minimum $_ - -	Maximum $_ _ -
		Maximum $_ - -	Minimum $_ _ -
Total	$_ - -	Minimum $_ - -	Maximum $_ _ -
		Maximum $_ - -	Minimum $_ - -

(1) The several Underwriters have agreed to purchase any unsubscribed shares at the Subscription Price. See "Underwriting" herein for details as to the method of computing underwriting commissions, the assumptions on which the minimum and maximum commissions and the corresponding proceeds to the Company shown above are calculated, and the obligation of the Underwriters under certain circumstances to pay to the Company any net profit realized upon the sale of unsubscribed shares. The Company has agreed to indemnify the Underwriters against certain civil liabilities, including liabilities under the Securities Act of 1933.

(2) Before deducting expenses payable by the Company estimated at $

During and after the subscription period, the several Underwriters may offer shares of Common Stock (including shares acquired or to be acquired by them through the purchase and exercise of Rights or otherwise, some of which Rights may be purchased from stockholders referred to under "Principal Stockholders" herein) to the public at prices set from time to time by the Representative of the Underwriters, it being contemplated that an offering price set in any calendar day will not be increased more than once during such day. Such prices will be not less than the Subscription Price per share set forth above (less, in the case of sales to dealers, any concession allowed to dealers) and not more than either the last sale price or the current offering price on the New York Stock Exchange, whichever is higher, plus an amount equal to the applicable New York Stock Exchange commission. The Underwriters may thus realize profits or losses independent of the underwriting compensation stated above.

Kuhn, Loeb & Co.

November   , 1958.

The SEC requires a detailed report before it accepts a new issue of securities for registration. A summary of the report must be included in the prospectus given to everyone offered the securities. Polaroid was offering its shareowners the right (see page 48) to buy additional stock.

the amount due on its cumulative preferred stock, the dividend is payable in the future. The company's obligation is not wiped out; it accumulates. All back dividends must be paid to holders of cumulative preferred stock before any dividend may be paid to the holders of the corporation's common stock.

Ordinarily, the voting rights of holders of preferred stock are limited to a few situations specified in the corporation's bylaws. Holders of common stock almost always have the right to vote for the corporation's board of directors and on matters for which their consent is required by law or by the corporation's own rules.

The agreement worked out between the Lands, Wheelwright, and the investment bankers provided that Polaroid Corporation would issue 7,500 shares of Cumulative Class A preferred stock with a stated value of $100 per share. The dividend rate was fixed at $5 a year. The bankers were to buy 3,750 shares of the Class A stock immediately and were to purchase the remaining half within two years if the corporation called upon them to do so. When Polaroid required additional capital, the bankers bought the second half of the Class A stock.

The Lands and Wheelwright were paid with stock for the value of their business and its patents. They received all the Cumulative Class B preferred stock consisting of 2,500 shares with a stated value of $5 per share. Yearly dividends were fixed at $5 but were due only after dividends on Class A stock had been paid.

The Lands and Wheelwright also got all of Polaroid's common stock consisting of 100,000 shares. The assigned value was $1 per share.

Thus the corporation's capital, at the outset, was $487,500—the $375,000 paid by the investment bankers for the Cumulative Class A preferred stock and $112,500, the value assigned to the patents and business of the Land-Wheelwright companies and represented by the 2,500 shares of Cumulative Class B preferred stock and 100,000 shares of common stock. The bankers paid for their stock in cash; the Lands and Wheelwright paid for their stock by giving the new corporation the assets of their old companies. Such a financial arrangement is usual when an existing business is taken over by a new corporation.

Land signed a contract providing that he was to serve as head of Polaroid for ten years and that any inventions he patented during that period would belong to the corporation. It was also agreed that representatives of the investment bankers would be elected to Polaroid's board of directors, thus giving the bankers a voice in the operation of the company. Many companies make such agreements with their bankers.

The men who financed Polaroid Corporation believed, as did Land, that its most profitable business would be the sale of headlight filters. Although there was no filtering material that could compete with Land's, another company held six patents for light polarization. Polaroid's stockholders voted to buy that company to obtain its patents. The price paid was $25,000 in cash and 7,000 shares of common stock in Polaroid Corporation. These shares were issued for the purpose of making the purchase and brought the number of Polaroid's common stock to 107,000.

When a company issues additional stock, every one of its shares represents a smaller part of the business. If a company has ten shares of common stock outstanding, each represents one-tenth of the business. If ten more shares are issued, each represents one-twentieth of the business. The effect is the same as if a cake was first cut into ten pieces and then each piece was cut in half. By increasing the number of slices, the size of each is decreased.

However, when the number of shares in a company is increased and at the same time something of value is added to the business, the original shareowners may be in a better position than they were before. Polaroid's shareowners believed that by issuing the additional common stock to buy the other company, they were making their business more valuable.

Actually, little was gained by the purchase, for Polaroid never sold headlight filters. Automobile manufacturers maintained that it was impractical to put filters on new cars because old cars would not be so equipped.

Shortly before the United States entered World War II, George Wheelwright, who had started in business with Land and had received stock in Polaroid Corporation when it was organized, became an officer in the Navy. While settling his business affairs, Wheelwright sold 235 shares of his common stock in Polaroid Corporation to security dealers. They paid between $45-$55 a share. Wheelwright's sale and sales by other stockholders resulted in shares in Polaroid Corporation becoming available to the general public.

Polaroid Corporation did not become a real moneymaker until Dr. Land invented the camera that has revolutionized photography. He credits his daughter with sparking the camera idea. The girl had posed for snapshots and wanted to see the pictures right away. Her father explained that cameras performed only one step in picture making—the exposure of the film. He said that developing film and making prints from it were separate operations carried out after the film was removed from the camera. Having given this explanation, Dr. Land thought that it should be possible to design a camera capable of producing a finished print. He started to work on inventing such a camera in 1944.

In 1945 the company reported earnings of over $400,-000, but dividends on its preferred stock were in arrears. Polaroid's board of directors proposed changes in the company's capital structure, and they were approved by the stockholders. During the month of September, the dividend arrears were wiped out by the issuance of new preferred stock to replace the old.

At the same time, a change was made in the company's common stock. Holders were given three shares of the new common stock for each share of their old. Such a distribution is known as a three-for-one split. Stockholders are usually pleased with stock splits, although actually they do not increase their interest in the company. If an investor has 100 shares in a corporation with 100,000 shares outstanding, he owns 1/1000 of the corporation. If the stock is split three for one, he has 300 of the company's 300,000 shares and he still owns 1/1000 of the corporation.

One reason why companies split their stock is to bring

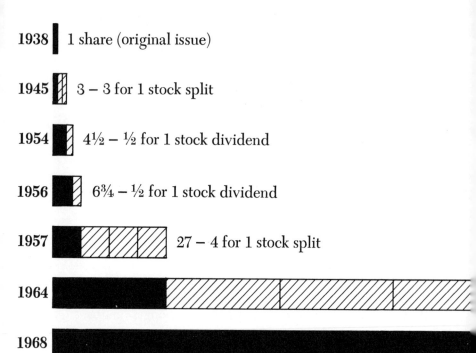

1938 — 1 share (original issue)

1945 — 3 – 3 for 1 stock split

1954 — 4½ – ½ for 1 stock dividend

1956 — 6¾ – ½ for 1 stock dividend

1957 — 27 – 4 for 1 stock split

1964

1968

its market price into a comparatively low range. Many investors will not, or cannot, buy stock selling in a high price range. Assume that stock selling at $100 a share is split three for one. Ordinarily, its market price would fall to a fraction over $33. At that price more buyers may be attracted, and as a result of their buying, the market price of the stock may go up to $35 or $37. Then a person who owned the stock before the split-up has a more valuable investment, and if he sells, can make a profit.

Sometimes companies give their stockholders stock as

POLAROID CORPORATION

This chart shows how one share purchased in 1938 grew in 30 years to 216 shares.

108 − 4 for 1 stock split

216 − 2 for 1 stock split

dividends. A stock dividend may be declared instead of a cash dividend, but frequently it is in addition to a cash payment. Stock dividends are very similar to stock splits. From an investor's point of view, both have the same effect. He gets additional shares of stock. He usually gets fewer shares from a stock dividend than from a stock split. A company may declare a 2 percent stock dividend, in which case stockholders get two additional shares for each hundred that they own. When the stock dividend to which a shareholder is entitled does not work out to a whole number of shares, the value of the additional fraction of a share is usually paid for by check.

From 1945 to 1968, Polaroid split its stock a number of times and also paid a number of stock dividends. As a result, each share grew in the twenty-three years to 216 shares. And the market value of a share in Polaroid Corporation increased tremendously, due to the great success of Polaroid cameras.

As part of its financial plan of 1945, Polaroid issued and sold 80,875 additional shares of common stock for $28 a share. Polaroid's stockholders were given the first opportunity to buy the new shares. Such an opportunity is known as a "right." In some cases the law requires that newly issued stock be offered first to the company's stockholders.

A right is usually worth money. The new stock is generally offered at a lower price than the company's outstanding stock is selling for in the market. If the market price is $25, the new stock may be offered at $23.50. Thus, on each share of the new stock that an investor is entitled to buy, he may be able to make $1.50 Usually, for stock listed by the big stock markets, he need not go to the trouble of buying shares from the company and then selling them at the market. He can sell his rights at the exchange where the company's stock is traded.

Polaroid's story is unique in many respects, but its financial history is similar to that of many other large corporations. In the beginning the founders of a business provide the capital; then, in order to obtain money for expansion, shares are sold to investment bankers; and the third step is the marketing of shares to the public.

5

THE MARKET WITHOUT
A MARKETPLACE

When shares in Polaroid Corporation were first offered to the public, the sales were made in the over-the-counter market. The securities of young companies are never traded at organized stock exchanges. They are bought and sold over-the-counter.

The term, over-the-counter, was an accurate description when it was first used back in colonial days. Then merchants and bankers bought and sold securities over the counters of their establishments. That system became outmoded long ago. Today most over-the-counter business is done by telephone.

A far greater number of securities are traded over-the-counter than at organized exchanges. Most bonds issued by the federal government and by states and cities are bought and sold over-the-counter. The same is true of the stocks and bonds of many large corporations, including some of the country's biggest banks and insurance companies.

But it is for small companies that the over-the-counter market is of greatest importance. Companies whose volume of business or number of shareholders does not qualify them for listing by an organized stock exchange depend on the over-the-counter market; without it there would be no trading in such securities.

Although trading is no longer done over counters, the basic system is unchanged. When merchants dealt in securities, they bought for their own account from people who wished to sell, and they sold from their inventory of securities to people who wished to buy. The merchants made a profit by selling securities at a higher price than the securities had cost them. Many modern over-the-counter security dealers operate in the same way.

A broker who fills an order at a stock market acts as his customer's agent. The broker bargains for his customer and is paid a commission for his services. Over-the-counter transactions may also be handled on a brokerage basis. Then the commissions charged are usually in accordance with the rate schedule of the New York Stock Exchange.

But many over-the-counter transactions are made on a dealer basis. When a security dealer sells to a customer, or buys from him, the dealer is acting for himself. He does not charge a commission; he hopes to make a profit on the transaction, and it is included in the price he names. Many firms that handle over-the-counter securities act sometimes as brokers, sometimes as dealers.

No dealer can keep a supply of all of the thousands of securities now traded over-the-counter. If a dealer does not have the stock that a customer wishes, he buys it from another dealer and resells it to his customer. A dealer does not make telephone calls at random to locate a source from which he can obtain any particular stock. Dealers who make a market for the securities of certain companies, that is, who will either buy or sell them, are listed in a daily publication known as "the pink sheets" because they are printed on pink paper. The listings include each of the dealer's quoted selling and buying prices and his telephone number. Some stocks are handled by only one dealer, but a number of dealers may be listed for others. When there is competition among dealers, some offer better terms than others.

Prices quoted in the pink sheets are only approximations. In other words, they are bargaining figures. When filling an order, conscientious dealers do some telephone shopping to find from which market-maker the best price can be obtained. A dealer who buys at the best possible price can give his customer a favorable price.

Since all over-the-counter transactions are privately negotiated between dealers, or between dealers and their customers, actual prices are not reported as they are of transactions at stock exchanges. The only information about prices supplied to the public is contained in the tabulations prepared by the National Association of Security Dealers. The tabulations are published in the financial sections of newspapers and give, for selected securities, average prices at which dealers have bought or sold to each other. Newspapers give the source of the tabulations and state, in an explanatory paragraph, what the prices represent. The *New York Times'* explanation is typical. It says:

"Quotations supplied by the National Association of Security Dealers are representative inter-dealer prices as of approximately 3 P.M. (the previous day). Inter-dealer markets change throughout the day. Prices do not include retail markup, markdown, or commissions."

Although they do not give the prices at which the public has bought or sold, the tabulations are a useful guide for investors. The quotations tell an investor about what he will have to pay if he buys and about how much he will get if he sells. Before over-the-counter quotations were published, the public had no way of knowing whether a price named by a dealer was or was not fair.

Only dealers who are members of the National Association of Security Dealers can trade with members at inter-dealer prices. Nonmembers get no price advantage over the general public. This restriction is imposed to make membership in the Association a business necessity. In the usual situation, a securities dealer must buy or sell at inter-dealer prices in order to make a profit on his business with the public.

The Association was organized under a provision of the law Congress enacted in 1938 for the regulation of the over-the-counter market. Instead of making the government solely responsible for establishing and enforcing regulations, the law authorized the formation of dealers' associations to share in performing the regulatory duties. Only one organization, the National Association of Security Dealers, has been established. The NASD's rules as to what members may and may not do are drafted in consultation with the Securities and Exchange Commission.

One of the first problems that the Association tackled was dealers' charges. At a stock exchange it takes no more time for a broker to buy shares in Company A than in Company B. Commission rates can therefore be standardized. But in the over-the-counter market, some transactions take far more time and effort than others. If a dealer sells shares that he owns, all he need do is to take them from his supply. Or if a customer orders stock in which there is active trading, his dealer merely phones a few sources to find from which one he can get the best price. But if a dealer is asked to buy or to sell shares in a little known company located in a town a thousand or more miles away, he may spend considerable time to complete the transaction.

A survey made by the NASD disclosed that in 71 percent of the transactions reported by members, 5 percent or less had been added to the wholesale price as the charge for the dealer's services. The Association thereupon adopted 5 percent as the base for determining a fair charge. It stated that in some cases a higher fee than 5 percent might be justified, and in other cases a lower fee would be proper. To guide its members, the Association includes in its manual pages of facts that dealers are to take into consideration.

Members' business records are checked periodically by the Association's inspectors to determine whether the NASD's rules and the law have been complied with. In addition to any violations the inspectors may report, complaints may be filed with the Association by one member against another, or by the public. The alleged violator is sent a copy of the report, and either he or the complainant may ask for a hearing by the NASD's local Business Conduct Committee. If it decides that a violation has occurred, it names the penalty for the offense.

Decisions of local committees are subject to review by the NASD's Board of Governors. The most severe penalty the board can impose is expulsion from the Association.

The Securities and Exchange Commission not only has authority to review decisions of the NASD but may also proceed directly against members. In some cases it has increased the penalties imposed by the Association by revoking dealers' official registration certificates. Such a revocation bars a man from engaging in the security business.

Policing the over-the-counter market is far more difficult than the policing of stock exchanges. However, the SEC's policing has become more effective since it installed a computer to act as a watchdog. The computer "remembers" the price range over a period of several years of the more than 8,000 stocks listed in the pink sheets and prints out an alert when there is any considerable change in the price pattern of a stock. The change may indicate that manipulators are working on the stock. The SEC finds out by investigating. Investigation is also prompt when the computer reports activity in a stock that has not been traded in for some time. The investigators may find that there are valid reasons for the revival of interest in the stock. But they may also uncover a dealer's scheme to make money by selling stock he acquired for pennies in a company whose financial condition is shaky.

In recent years government control of the over-the-counter market has been expanded. Prior to 1964, companies whose securities were traded over-the-counter were exempt from the disclosure requirements with which companies listed on organized exchanges had to comply. Now similar rules apply to both. Over-the-counter companies that have assets of $1,000,000 or more and 500 or more shareowners must make periodic reports to the SEC of their financial position, the names of officers and directors, the number of shares they own, and so on. Shareholders in the companies must be given a full financial report each year.

The 1964 law gives the Commission the power to suspend trading in the securities of an over-the-counter company. Previously, it could halt trading only of securities sold at stock markets. One of the first suspensions ordered in over-the-counter trading was of shares in an oil company. The company's annual report disclosed an unfavorable condition, and the Commission ordered a five-day suspension in trading in the company's stock so that dealers and the public would have time to learn of the situation.

6

INSIDE VIEW OF A
STOCKBROKER'S OFFICE

You don't have to be a customer or even a prospective customer to go into a stockbroker's office. The public is welcome, and in many brokerage offices a free show can be viewed. From 10 A.M. to 3:30 P.M., New York time, while the nation's two largest stock markets are open for trading, reports of sales concluded minutes before are projected on screens.

One projecting system produces a parade of figures moving from right to left across a narrow screen. Another system projects the figures in columnar form. Formerly, stock market transactions were recorded on paper tape by the telegraphic printing device called a ticker. Every brokerage office had one or more tickers, and miles of printed tape were produced every day. It was the custom

56

in New York City, when visiting celebrities were driven up Broadway, to toss streamers of ticker tape from skyscraper windows. The effect was dramatic, but a squad of street cleaners had to be sent out to remove the litter.

To read ticker tape, a person had to stand at the ticker and watch the reports as they were printed. Only a few people could read the tape at the same time. The projected reports, one of New York Stock Exchange transactions and a second of American Stock Exchange transactions, can be seen by everyone in a brokerage office. Members of the staff can watch them without moving from their desks; chairs are usually lined up directly in front of the screens for members of the public.

Each report starts with a code letter or a group of letters identifying the company whose stock was traded. The exchange on which the company is listed assigns the code letters. Some are easy to recognize—GE, for instance, is General Electric, and GM, General Motors Corporation. But many of the letters have no relationship to the name of the company. To find out what the code letters stand for, you look in a code symbol book. Some brokerage offices keep a copy of the book on a rack for the use of visitors, and other offices supply it upon request. Most people who regularly watch market reports know the code letters of the companies in which they are interested.

The prices at which stocks have been sold are given in whole numbers and fractions. The dollar sign is omitted. Therefore, 20¾ means a price of $20.75 per share and 58⅞ a price of $58.875. If only a price figure is given,

100 shares were traded. If the transaction involved 200 shares, the price figure is preceded by 2s, a sale of 300 shares by 3s, and so on up to 900. For 1,000 shares or more, the number is given in full.

In addition to the data projected on the screens, brokerage offices also have "quote boards" on which more detailed information is shown. Before electrically controlled quote boards were developed, blackboards were used for displaying the trading statistics for selected companies. The blackboards usually showed the first price at which the company's stock was sold that day, the highest and lowest prices paid during the day, and the price of the most recent sale. A man known as a board marker erased the old figures and wrote in new ones as prices changed. Brokers' offices are still called board rooms because of the old blackboards.

Since the introduction of electrical quote boards, more information about more securities can be given than was possible on blackboards. Quote boards are composed of a series of narrow panels, each company having one panel. At the top of it, the company's name is indicated by its code letters. In addition to the prices for the day, the board may show the price range for the year.

When a customer telephones his broker's office and asks about a "boarded" stock (one included on the quote board), the man who is handling his account can usually get the answer by glancing at the board. If it does not contain the desired price information, he can obtain it by a direct query to a computer center. The New York Stock Exchange's computers give voice answers to telephoned requests for price quotations. Members of the Exchange

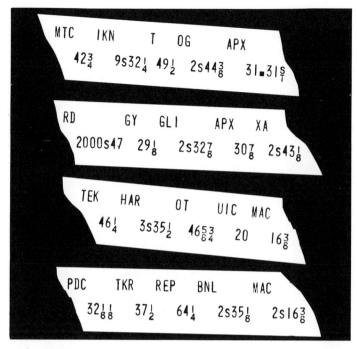

MTC	IKN		T	OG	APX
$42\frac{3}{4}$	$9s32\frac{1}{4}$		$49\frac{1}{2}$	$2s44\frac{3}{8}$	$31\blacksquare31\frac{s}{1}$

RD		GY	GLI	APX	XA	
$2000s47$		$29\frac{1}{8}$		$2s32\frac{7}{8}$	$30\frac{7}{8}$	$2s43\frac{1}{8}$

TEK	HAR		OT	UIC	MAC
$46\frac{1}{4}$	$3s35\frac{1}{2}$		$46\frac{53}{84}$	20	$16\frac{3}{8}$

PDC	TKR	REP	BNL		MAC
$32\frac{11}{88}$	$37\frac{1}{2}$	$64\frac{1}{4}$	$2s35\frac{1}{8}$		$2s16\frac{3}{8}$

Market transactions are projected in code. MTC is Monsanto Company. The sale of 100 shares was at $42.75 per share. The 9s below IKN (Interlaken Steel Corporation) means a sale of 900 shares, and the 32¼ a price of $32.25. Code symbol books list the abbreviations for company names.

who subscribe to its "voice answer back" service have a special phone hook-up with the computers. By dialing the appropriate code, an answer can be obtained as to the price situation of any one of the stocks listed on the Exchange. The computers can handle as many as 400,000 queries a day.

Many brokerage firms have desk-size instruments that show price quotations visually. One named "Telequote" has a two-inch television screen. The instrument is connected with a central data system that can supply quotations on stocks traded at the country's major exchanges and in the over-the-counter market. To get the desired information, one must press certain keys, and the data appears on the screen.

Unlike the system at banks where any teller can cash a customer's check or accept his deposit, brokerage firms assign one member of their staff to each customer. Various titles are used for these staff members. Some brokerage firms call them account executives, others customers' brokers, and still others registered representatives. The last is the most accurate, for these staff members must be registered, that is, be licensed by the Securities and Exchange Commission, and they are representatives of their firm. Most investors, however, refer to the person with whom they deal as their broker. He takes their orders and answers their questions.

There are many reasons for choosing one brokerage firm instead of another, but the cost of the service does not affect the decision. All brokerage firms charge exactly the same fee for buying or selling at exchanges. The exchanges fix the fees. The established fees are the minimum commissions that may be charged. However, competition for the public's business has resulted in brokers charging no more than the minimum rate.

The schedule of the New York Stock Exchange provides for a commission of 6 percent on transactions involving $100 or less. The rate of commissions decreases as the amount involved in a transaction increases. On purchases or sales totaling $2,400 to $4,999.99, commis-

Typical application form for a brokerage account.

sions are one-half of 1 percent plus $19. Thus, for a purchase of 100 shares at $24 each, the brokerage commission would be $31 (one half of 1 percent of $2,400 = $12 + $19).

61

Brokerage firms hope that some of the people who come into their offices to watch the market news will become customers. They also advertise their services. But they do not accept everyone who says he wants to be a customer. The applicant must be over twenty-one, show that he is in a sound financial position, and has a reputation for paying his bills, for brokerage firms extend credit to their customers.

When a customer gives an order to buy stock, the brokerage firm buys immediately and is responsible for the payment of the purchase price. Ordinarily, the customer need not pay until four days later when the stock certificates are delivered to the brokerage firm. If the customer fails to pay and the price of the stock falls, the brokerage firm could lose considerable money.

As a practical matter, customers cannot make an immediate cash payment. Not only are many orders given by telephone, but even if a customer is at his brokerage office when he gives his order, neither he nor his registered representative knows, in most instances, the amount of the bill. Assume that the last sale of the stock the customer orders was made at $15.25 a share. The customer is willing to buy at about that price and orders 100 shares "at the market," which means at the best price obtainable when the order is filled. The price may be a little more or a little less than that of the preceding sale.

During the first discussion with a new customer, he may be asked if he wishes the brokerage firm to act as custodian of the securities it purchases for him. If he requests this service, the securities are purchased in the name of the brokerage firm. This arrangement is known as buying in a "street name."

The big advantage to a customer of buying in a street name is that he is relieved of the care of his securities. Customers are sent monthly statements listing the securities held for them, any dividends received on them, and the amount paid for securities that have been sold. All money received for a customer is credited to his account unless he directs it be paid to him immediately. Money in a customer's account is applied to the next purchase he makes.

Both for a brokerage firm and for a customer the street-name arrangement is convenient when securities are sold. Delivery of securities, like payment for those purchased, must be made within four days after the sale. When a brokerage firm has the securities in its vault, it takes care of all the details involved in delivering them. An investor who buys in his own name and has possession of his securities must go to his bank, remove the ones he has sold from his safe-deposit box (securities should never be kept in a desk, dresser, or file), properly endorse the securities, and send them to the brokerage firm by registered mail or by a responsible messenger. All of this bother, and the expense of renting a safe-deposit box, can be eliminated by buying in a street name.

Why doesn't everyone take advantage of a brokerage firm's offer of custodian service? Usually for one of two reasons. Some people enjoy having physical possession of their securities; other people are concerned about the safety of having their brokerage firm, instead of themselves, named as the owner. Actually, the situation is much the same as when money is deposited in a bank. The banker has possession of the money; the person to whom it belongs has merely the bank's record of the amount in his account.

Brokerage firms are closely regulated. They are prohibited from making any use of securities customers leave with them unless specifically authorized to do so. In addition to official inspections, the exchange or association of which the brokerage firm is a member checks its books and records. No advance notice is given of when an inspection will be made; books and records may be called for at any time. Not long ago the largest brokerage firm in the United States advertised that a surprise audit of its business had recently been completed. The advertisement stated:

"The New York Stock Exchange requires that every member firm doing business with the public be subject to a surprise audit during the year.

"Our audit is a big job. At the peak more than 370 auditors were at work in New York and our larger offices. Among other things, they carefully counted all of the securities in our vault—more than 43,000 separate issues worth about $12.5 billion.

"As a vital part of the audit, 631,000 regular customers received confirming notices of their accounts."

Reputable brokerage firms—the only kind with which anyone should do business—take pride in their good name and in the reputation of the security business as a whole.

7

BONDS ARE IOU'S

Not long ago the Chicago City School District needed $25,000,000 to build schools. The money was raised by the sale of bonds. If Mr. John Citizen wants a loan to pay for re-roofing his house, for instance, he goes to his bank. Cities, states, and the federal government, as well as business companies, obtain the vast loans they need by selling bonds.

When a bank makes a loan to Mr. Citizen, it requires him to sign an agreement that he will repay the money by a specified date and that until then he will pay interest at a specified rate. Bonds are far more elaborate documents than the simple agreements that bind an individual to repay a debt, but their purpose and effect is the same. Bonds are IOU's.

Most individuals are obliged to pledge something of value in order to obtain a loan. Mr. Citizen's bank, for example, might require him to give it a mortgage on his home. If he fails to make the payments provided for in his agreement, the bank can, through legal proceedings, sell Mr. Citizen's home to get back its money. Some business corporations also give a mortgage on their property as security for their bonds. But many bonds issued by corporations, and all United States bonds, are backed by nothing but the promise of the borrower to repay. Such bonds, when issued by corporations, are known as debentures.

There is a lot to read on a bond. The face value of the bond—how much the borrower is to pay when the bond becomes due—is printed in large type. The number of the bond, the name of the bond issue, and the date when the loan will mature are given in the heading. The maturity, or expiration date of a bond, is generally in the far distant future. Many bonds are not payable for twenty years, thirty years, or more.

In the following paragraphs, the borrower's obligations and rights are summarized. The borrower may have the right to prepay the loan. When bonds are redeemed before their maturity date, the borrower is sometimes obliged, under the terms stated on the bond, to pay more than its full value.

You might think that bondholders would be glad to get the additional money, but this frequently is not the fact. The right to prepay bonds is to the advantage of the borrower.

Companies advertise when they prepay bonds. Those listed by Sinclair were chosen by lot from the entire issue.

No. M

GOVERNMENT

OF

NEW ZEALAND

TWELVE YEAR

6¾% BOND

DUE

JULY 15, 1979

INTEREST PAYABLE

JANUARY 15 AND
JULY 15

PRINCIPAL AND INTEREST PAYABLE
IN THE
BOROUGH OF MANHATTAN,
CITY AND STATE OF NEW YORK,
UNITED STATES OF AMERICA
AND AT PAYING AGENCIES
APPOINTED BY NEW ZEALAND

DE LA RUE BANKNOTE COMPANY

Bonds are usually folded so that a section of the back serves as a cover (left). Each coupon attached to a bearer bond is numbered and states the date when interest is payable and the amount due (above). Bonds contain a detailed description of the terms that the borrower is to fulfill. The rights of bondholders are also set forth. The first four coupons have been clipped from this bond (right).

The rate of interest that a borrower must pay to obtain a loan is higher at some times than at others. If bonds are issued when interest rates are high and subsequently they drop, borrowers can save money by calling in their bonds and issuing new ones providing for a lower interest rate. Even though holders of the old bonds are paid a premium, they are not financially in as good a position as

they would have been if the bonds had not been redeemed. It is unlikely that the money can be reinvested at as high an interest rate as was payable on the old bonds.

People frequently talk of the amount of the interest due on bonds as the coupon rate. It's an appropriate term because many bonds are issued with interest coupons attached. Each coupon is dated and states, in dollars and cents, how much interest is payable. When payments are due, the bondholder clips the coupon and gives it to his bank or brokerage firm for collection. Coupons are made out to the "bearer," and anyone can cash them. Bonds with coupons attached are known as bearer bonds.

If a thief steals a bearer bond, its owner is in as bad a spot as if he had been robbed of money. If the thief is caught with the bond in his possession, it will be returned to the rightful owner. But thieves quickly dispose of their loot. And after a thief sells a bearer bond, the person to whom it belonged loses his right to reclaim it.

Bond owners can—and many do—protect themselves against the risk of loss from theft or the destruction of their bonds by fire or other causes by registering their

The name of the owner is written on a registered bond in the position where the word specimen appears. Registration affords protection if a bond is lost, destroyed, or stolen.

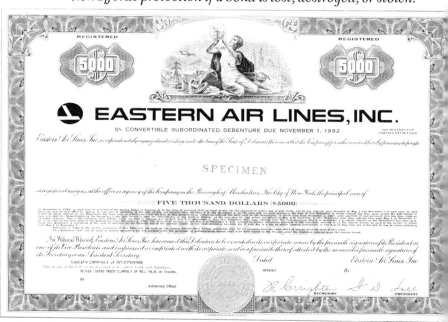

bonds with the company or governmental agency that issued them. No charge is made for registration. It includes recording the bondholder's name and address and replacing his bearer bond with a registered bond on which the owner's name is written. This is only the beginning of the bookkeeping job, for a registered bond has no coupons attached. When interest payments are due, checks must be mailed to each registered bondholder. Making payments on coupons is far easier.

United States Series E Savings Bonds, with which most people are familiar, are registered when sold. The owner's name is typed on the bond. In three respects E bonds are in a class by themselves.

First, they are issued in smaller denominations than other bonds. E bonds start at $25. Corporate bonds ordinarily have a minimum face value of $1,000.

Second, until a Series E bond matures, or is redeemed (that is, turned in to the government for cash), its owner does not receive any interest. The bond is bought for less than its matured value. You pay $18.75 for a $25 bond. The $6.25 difference is the interest payable when the bond matures. Interest at a lower rate is paid if an E bond is not held for its full term. A schedule of interest paid for each six-month period is given on the bond.

The third way in which Series E bonds are different from others is that they cannot be sold by an owner to another person. An owner who wishes to dispose of his bond can get cash for it only in accordance with the government's redemption provisions.

E bonds can be redeemed at any post office, bank, or office of the United States Treasury Department. However, before cash is paid for an E bond, the person presenting it must identify himself as its owner or show that he has been authorized by the owner to present the bond.

Brokers handle the sale of other registered bonds in much the same way as bearer bonds. However, the registered owner must sign a paper transferring ownership, and the company or governmental unit that issued the bond must be given the signed paper so that it can change its records. Just as when a bond is first registered, no charge is made for recording a change in ownership. It is the custom to give this service, although the issuer of a bond neither profits nor loses when it is resold.

The United States government tops the list of bond issuers. It may obtain a loan of more than a billion dollars from the sale of one bond issue. Yet even such a large issue may be oversubscribed. Comparatively recently, the United States offered a $1,600,000,000 bond issue and received so many orders that only about 10 percent of them could be filled. The money obtained from purchasers of these bonds was used by the government to repay its debt on the maturity date of previously issued bonds. The issuance of new bonds to obtain funds to pay money due on other bonds is a standard financing procedure known as a refunding operation.

When the United States borrows, the Treasury Department decides the amount of the loan desired, the period it will run, and the rate of interest that will be paid. Following these decisions, the government has bonds prepared and offers them for sale.

A different system is used by states, cities, other governmental agencies, and business corporations. Ordinar-

Minnesota School Unit Rejects 2 Bids on Issue

By a WALL STREET JOURNAL *Staff Reporter*

MINNEAPOLIS — Bloomington Independent School District No. 271, Hennepin and Scott Counties, Minn., rejected the only two bids submitted for $3.5 million building bonds.

The best bidder was a group led by Piper, Jaffray & Hopwood, John Nuveen & Co. and Juran & Moody, Inc., with a proposed annual net interest cost of 4.44%, followed by Ebin, Robertson & Co., with a 4.58% cost basis.

The district rejected the proposals, said T. G. Evensen, president of T. G. Evensen & Associates, financial advisers, because of the limited competition, and "the wide spread in net interest cost which indicated dealer uncertainty as to market conditions."

Board members of the district are scheduled to meet June 1 to consider alternate financing plans, Mr. Evensen said. Possible alternatives include sale of the issue through direct negotiations and deferment of the financing for "possibly two or three months."

ily, they sell their bonds to investment bankers. The bankers underwrite the loan, that is, they pay for the entire bond issue and assume the risk that they will be able to resell the bonds at a profit. Since the bankers' purchase price may be many millions, one firm of investment bankers rarely underwrites a bond issue by itself. The bankers organize a group, and each member of it agrees to pay for a certain percentage of the bonds.

Bond issues are usually sold to investment bankers at a discount. In other words, the borrower gets less from the bankers than it will have to pay when the bonds become due. Naturally, corporations and governmental agencies want to get the highest possible price for their bonds. Sometimes they "shop around" to find which investment bankers will give the most favorable terms, and sometimes the choice of investment bankers is determined by competitive bidding. Competitive bidding is required by law for some government and corporation bond issues. Ordinarily, the highest bid is accepted. But the rules governing a competition may provide that all bids may be rejected as unsatisfactory. In such a situation, a prospective borrower usually waits for a while and then asks for the submission of new bids. At the time of the second bidding, a change in general financial conditions may result in a higher price being offered for a bond issue.

An agreement by investment bankers to purchase a bond issue is not immediately followed by an offering of the bonds to the public. Authorization to sell corporate bonds must be obtained from the Security and Exchange Commission. The text that is to appear on the bonds must be prepared and approved by lawyers. The printing and engraving of the bonds also takes time.

When bonds of a new issue are first offered to the public, their price is fixed by the group of investment bankers marketing them. All buyers pay the same price, no matter which firm of bankers they deal with. By agreement the bankers maintain the fixed price for a certain period. Afterwards, the price depends on what a buyer is willing to pay and a seller is willing to take.

The price of bonds fixed by a group of investment bankers may be higher than the face value of the bonds.

74

If at a time when most bond issues are yielding interest at 5 percent, bonds backed by an established company are offered at a 5¼ percent rate of interest, they are obviously more desirable and therefore can be sold at a premium price.

Often bonds given a high rating by one of the organizations that specialize in financial analysis are priced above their face value. The analysts consider the entire financial structure of the bond issuer, its income, debts, the source from which it will obtain the money to make payments on the bonds, and so forth. The ratings indicate the relative safety of bond issues, that is, how certain an investor can be of receiving his full interest and the return of his money when the bond is due.

Moody's Investors Service was the first to publish bond ratings. Moody's started in 1909 to indicate its opinion of the quality of bonds by letters: top grade is Aaa, second grade is Aa, third grade A. B, C, and D are also divided into three categories. The lowest rating given is D. Another organization, Standard and Poor's, also uses alphabetical designations for its grading. It uses all capital letters, AAA, AA, A, and so on to D. These two leading rating organizations do not always agree on the quality of a bond issue. One may rate a bond issue higher than the other. So important are ratings in the sale of bonds that even before they are accepted for registration by the Securities and Exchange Commission, investment bankers frequently request ratings from Moody's and Standard and Poor's and supply them with the voluminous data they require.

8

TECHNIQUES USED
BY SPECULATORS

There are two points of view on buying securities, one is that of the investor, the other that of the speculator. The investor is interested in the safety of his capital and is satisfied with a comparatively small profit over a period of time. The speculator knowingly takes big risks in the hope of making big profits quickly.

Professional and amateur speculators operate quite differently. Speculation on the part of many amateurs is limited to the purchase of low-priced stock in companies without an established record as to earnings. Buying such stock does not require a large outlay, and there is a chance of a high percentage of profit. But there is a greater chance that the stock will decrease in value or become worthless.

Amateurs often buy on the basis of an "inside tip." Such tips are usually unreliable. People should be (but many are not) suspicious of tips supplied by strangers. Why should they give a tip unless they stand to gain by giving it? And if a tip comes from a friend, the question is where did he get it?

Government restrictions have severely limited one form of speculation—buying on margin—which in the past was popular with amateurs. A margin buyer pays cash for only part of the cost of his stock and gets a loan for the balance from his broker. The cash the buyer pays is his margin. Buying on margin gives speculators a chance to make bigger profits than if they paid all cash. Here's how.

Suppose a man has $6,000 for buying stock. He picks a company in which shares are selling at $100 each. If he buys on a 60 percent margin, that is, pays only 60 percent in cash, he can buy 100 shares. If the market price of the stock increases to $106 and the margin buyer sells, he will make $600 or a 10 percent profit.

Now if he had paid all cash, he could have bought only 60 shares of the $100 stock with his $6,000. If he sold when the price rose to $106, the profit on his 60 shares would amount to $360 or 6 percent.

Before 1929 a large proportion of the stock bought at the New York Stock Exchange was on margin. Margins as low as 10 percent were usual, and the chance of making a 100 or 200 percent profit was great because stock prices were moving up.

The stock market collapse of 1929 showed the hazard

of buying on a thin margin. When stock prices fell, brokers called upon their customers to put up more cash. The additional cash was demanded because the market value of the stock was no longer sufficient security for the broker's loan. If a customer could not pay the additional cash, the broker sold the stock to obtain the money he had loaned. Such sales caused a further slide in prices, and another group of margin buyers received calls from their brokers to put up more cash. By the time market prices dropped to their low point, over half a million people who had bought on margin had forfeited all of their stock.

To prevent any recurrence of the wild speculation of the 1920's, Congress provided that the Federal Reserve Board fix the percentage of the purchase price of stocks bought at exchanges that must be paid in cash. Margin buying of securities sold in the over-the-counter market is prohibited. In the ten years between 1957 and 1967, margin requirements for purchases at exchanges ranged between 50–90 percent. For most of the period, a 70 percent margin was required.

In addition to the government's regulation of margin buying, it is also restricted by the rules of stock exchanges. The New York Stock Exchange specifies not only the amount of the buyer's initial payment but also the balance he must maintain as long as he holds stock on margin. To buy on margin, a speculator must deposit with his broker a minimum of $2,000 in cash or securities worth considerably more. The broker must call for more margin if the market price of the stock falls to a point at which, if the speculator sold and paid his broker's loan, he would have left less than 25 percent of the proceeds of the sale.

When stock is bought on margin, the broker keeps the stock certificates and, in accordance with the terms of the contract he makes with the buyer, has the right to pledge or, as the contract says, to hypothecate them. A broker may obtain a loan from a bank by pledging margined stocks as security. The broker, in turn, lends the money he has borrowed to his customers who want to buy on margin. Brokerage firms make a profit on such loans; they charge a higher rate of interest than they pay their bank.

Brokers also obtain a revenue from margined stock by lending it to people who sell "short." Speculators sell short, that is, they sell stock they do not own in the expectation of profiting from a fall in its price. As an example of this risky and fascinating maneuver, suppose a speculator believes that the price of XX Company stock will fall from its current price of $40 a share. The speculator telephones his broker and tells him to make a short sale of 100 shares in XX Company. A broker can't sell shares unless he can deliver them. The broker may have 100 shares of XX Company in one of his margin accounts that he can borrow and use for the short sale. Or he may borrow the stock from another broker.

When brokers lend stock, they are paid a cash sum equal to the value of the stock. (The money is obtained from the speculator's short sale of the stock.) The broker has the free use of the cash until he gets a replacement for the borrowed stock.

A speculator who sells short is required to deposit with

his broker the same amount as would be required if he were buying on margin. If the government's margin requirement is 70 percent, the short seller of XX Company at $4,000 would be obliged to deposit with his broker $2,800 or securities of that value.

If the speculator calculated correctly, the price of XX Company stock does fall. When the price goes down to $35, the short seller tells his broker to buy 100 shares of the stock. His buying price is $3,500, his selling price was $4,000. The speculator ends up with a $500 profit minus the various charges he is obligated to pay. The deal is completed when the stock that the speculator purchases is substituted for the stock that was borrowed.

But what happens if the speculator has figured wrong and instead of going down the price of XX stock goes up? That's the risk a short seller takes. In order to return the stock borrowed for the short sale, the speculator must pay the higher price at which it is selling in the market. If he were to buy at $45 a share, his loss would be $500 plus the commission payable to the broker and other expenses.

Speculators sometimes protect themselves against the possibility of a loss from a short sale by buying a "call." A call is a contract providing the right to buy a specified stock at a specified price within a specified period, 30 days, 60 days, 90 days, or longer.

Carrying our example of the speculator in XX Company stock one step further, assume that after his short sale he buys a 30-day call for 100 shares of XX stock. The speculator's broker arranges for the option contract with one of a small group of dealers who specialize in the option business. Prices of options vary according to the duration of the contract, the activity in the stock, and its market price. The speculator might pay about $250 for his option to buy XX stock at $40 a share. The price named in the contract is ordinarily the market price of the stock at the time the contract is made. If, within the 30 days covered by the option, the market price of the stock were to rise to $50, the speculator would exercise his option and buy at the lower price named in his contract to cover his short sale. In such a situation, a call serves a short seller as insurance against loss.

Speculators also buy calls (options to buy) and "puts" (options to sell) to attempt to make a profit from the up and down movement of the market. The cost of the option contract is the only money risked. A speculator who thinks that the price of a stock will go up buys a call. If he is right, he exercises his option, buys at his contract price, and makes a profit by selling the stock at the higher market price. If the price of the stock does not rise, the speculator lets his option lapse.

A speculator buys a put when he figures that the market price of a stock will fall. Such a contract gives a speculator the right to sell a stated number of shares within a certain time limit at a stated price, usually about the market price at the time the contract was made. If the price of the stock falls, the speculator buys it at the market price and sells in accordance with his put contract at the higher price named in it.

The advantage to speculators of buying puts and calls

Advertisement of a put and call dealer. "Close" tells the last price paid for the stock at the exchange on the preceding day. The second column of figures gives the price named in the contract. The date of its expiration is followed by the price of the option contract.

is obvious. But why should anyone be willing to give such contracts? The answer is that money can be made by doing it. Owners of large blocks of a company's stock find it advantageous to sell put and call contracts. They sell a put because they are willing to buy more of the company's stock; they sell a call because they are willing to sell some of their stock if called upon to do so.

Frequently put and call options are not exercised. The money paid to the party giving the option is all profit. But even if he fulfills the terms of the contract, his position is not unsatisfactory.

In our fictitious example of the call for 100 shares of XX Company stock, the person who agreed to sell at $40 a share received $225 for making the contract. (The additional $25 paid by the speculator was divided by the option dealer and the speculator's broker for their services.) If the speculator enforces his option contract, the party who gave it will actually be getting $42.25 a share, $2.25 from the payment for the option, and $40 for the stock. Of course he might have made more if he had sold at the market price. But on the whole, sellers of options are satisfied with their results. If they weren't, there would be no puts and calls.

Put and call contracts give professional speculators a chance to make large profits on a small investment. But such contracts are not for amateurs. For amateurs, any form of speculation is dangerous.

9

REPORTS TO
STOCKHOLDERS

About a hundred years ago, the New York Stock Exchange requested the companies whose stock was traded at the Exchange to publish financial reports of their operations. The only way of judging whether a company is doing well or badly is from figures that tell the amount of money it earned during a given period, what its expenses were, its profit, what it owns (assets), and what it owes (liabilities). Yet when the New York Stock Exchange made its request, few companies published the facts about their financial position. The Exchange received a sharp reply from one railroad company, which stated that it makes "no reports and publishes no statements."

Today every large corporation is required by law and also by the rules of stock exchanges to publish annual financial reports, and most companies report to share-owners four times a year. The reports covering a quarter of a year's operations are folders or small booklets, but annual reports covering a full year are usually large, handsome brochures. They are illustrated with photographs and drawings of the company's plants and products. Most companies print enough copies of their annual report so that they can send one to anyone who asks for it.

Generally, the first pages of an annual report are devoted to a summary of the company's record for the past year and its current plans. The summary is signed by the president of the company and also, in many cases, by the chairman of the board of directors.

After the introductory text come the vital portions of the report—the tabulations of the company's earnings for the year (its earning statement) and of its overall financial position (its balance sheet). With a little bit of study, you can understand the figures.

Companies are required to employ an independent firm of accountants to examine the figures and to certify that they fairly represent the financial position of the company. The firm of certified accountants is selected by the company's board of directors, subject to a vote of approval by shareowners. Years ago, as one book states, "considerable imagination" went into the preparation of financial reports. Now they are based on facts.

A company's financial condition is told by its balance sheet. It is a two-part tabulation. The part on the left is headed Assets, the one on the right Liabilities and Stockholders' Equity. Stockholders' equity is the stockholders' interest in the company—what is left after liabilities are subtracted from assets. Thus, the accounting system of listing liabilities and stockholders' equity on one side of a balance sheet and assets on the other results in both sides totaling the same. They are in balance, hence the term, balance sheet.

If you wanted to state your financial position as of today, you would start by listing your assets. First you would put down the cash in your pocket or pocketbook, next the amount of money you have in your savings bank account, then the dollar you lent a friend last week and expect him to repay next week, followed by the value of the things you own, bicycle, skates, typewriter, radio, etc. The same system is used by corporations.

First on a corporation's list of current assets is the cash it has in its own safe and in banks. Next are any securities that the company has purchased with its spare cash. The securities most frequently purchased by corporations are those issued by the United States government.

To carry on their business, many corporations must maintain an inventory of raw materials and also of finished products. The figure stating the value of a company's inventories can be used to determine the efficiency of its operation. More about this later.

The asset list includes an entry showing accounts receivable. The figure tells how much customers owe to the company for products that have been shipped to them or for services the company has rendered. Companies assume that all their bills will not be paid in full and therefore deduct a certain amount for nonpayments.

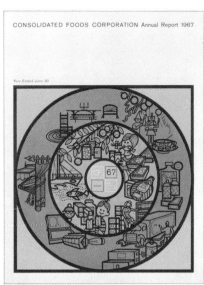

CONSOLIDATED FOODS CORPORATION Annual Report 1967

Year Ended June 30

Annual reports are handsome brochures.

Columbia Gas System
ANNUAL REPORT 1967

Squibb Beech-Nut, Inc. Annual Report 1967

Cash, securities that can readily be sold for cash, inventories, and accounts receivable are current assets. A second group includes the corporation's other assets. Among these are fixed assets—buildings, machinery, and other equipment, things intended for use and not to be turned into cash.

If you included in your list a fixed asset such as a typewriter or radio, what value would you put down for it? The amount it cost when new? But neither a radio, nor a typewriter, nor almost any other equipment is worth as much after use as when new. There is a depreciation in value due to wear and tear.

Accountants use standard methods for figuring depreciation. With the "straight-line" method, equal amounts are deducted each year during the expected useful life of a machine or other equipment.

Assume that a company buys a truck for $7,500 early in 1968 and its serviceability period is figured to be five years. One-fifth of the cost of the truck will be deducted each year. At the end of the first year, the value of the truck will be shown on the company's balance sheet as $6,000, and at the end of the second year, in 1970, as $4,500. In the 1973 balance sheet, the truck will not be listed. It will have been fully depreciated and for accounting purposes be without value. Actually, its useful life may be far from over. A new truck may not be required.

Patents that a company holds may also be included as assets, but frequently their true value is not indicated by the balance-sheet figure. For instance, all the patents held by Polaroid Corporation are listed at $1. The only purpose of such a listing is to show that a company has patents. Goodwill, that is, the value of a company's name and reputation, may also be listed as an asset. Some companies assign a large figure to goodwill, others only $1. For years General Motors Corporation's balance sheets have shown the value of its patents and goodwill as $63,-442,461.

Among the items listed as assets may be prepaid expenses. Such an item may be a payment for insurance. Many insurance policies cover a three-year period but are payable when they go into effect. Until the policy expires, the company has a credit for its advance payment.

The tabulation of liabilities usually starts with current liabilities. In this category are the amounts owing for supplies, wages, taxes, etc. When reading a balance sheet, you can get an important figure by subtracting current liabilities from current assets. The difference is the company's working capital, what it has to carry on its business.

Debts due after a year are listed as long-term liabilities. Under this heading you find the amount and description of any bonds that a company has outstanding.

Following the liability listings is the heading, stockholders' equity. The more descriptive term, stockholders' investment, is sometimes used, and the old-fashioned term, capital, is still found in some financial reports. They all mean the same thing—what stockholders own. In the itemization, any preferred stock that a company

GENERAL MOTORS CORPORATION
CONSOLIDATED BALANCE SHEET*
December 31, 1967

CURRENT ASSETS:

Cash	$ 402,592,113
Securities (United States bonds, foreign government bonds, etc., all short term)	1,399,904,333
Amounts owed to the corporation and its consolidated subsidiaries	1,833,583,767
Inventories (value of merchandise on hand)	3,210,408,568
TOTAL CURRENT ASSETS	6,846,488,781

INVESTMENTS AND MISCELLANEOUS ASSETS:

Value of General Motors' interest in subsidiary companies (not otherwise reflected in the consolidated statement, for example, General Motors Acceptance Corporation)	646,647,948
U.S. Government bonds maturing 1972	42,866,157
Other investments and miscellaneous assets	65,242,123
TOTAL INVESTMENTS AND MISCELLANEOUS ASSETS	754,756,228

COMMON STOCK IN TREASURY

Value of General Motors Corporation's own stock which it acquired (mostly for employee bonus plans and stock option plans)	149,414,069

REAL ESTATE, PLANTS, AND EQUIPMENT:

Cost of real estate, plants and equipment less depreciation	4,806,000,381
Cost of special tools less depreciation already deducted	526,998,289
TOTAL NET REAL ESTATE, PLANTS, AND EQUIPMENT	5,332,998,670

PREPAID EXPENSES (such as insurance premiums paid in advance)	125,982,310
GOODWILL, PATENTS, ETC.	63,442,466
TOTAL ASSETS	$13,273,082,524

*This tabulation is a slightly revised version of the one included in the corporation's Annual Report issued in 1968.

LIABILITIES, RESERVES, AND STOCKHOLDERS' EQUITY

CURRENT LIABILITIES:

Accounts payable (bills owed by General Motors)	$ 1,168,234,865
United States and foreign income taxes	527,865,820
Other taxes, payrolls, etc.	1,140,751,473
Dividends payable on preferred stocks	3,232,069
TOTAL CURRENT LIABILITIES	2,840,084,227
3⅛% Debenture bonds due 1979	42,813,000
FOREIGN DEBT OF SUBSIDIARIES DUE 1969-1992	302,013,100
OTHER LIABILITIES	589,802,310

(undelivered installments of bonus awards already earned, etc.)

RESERVES:

For various purposes such as the bonus plan, foreign operations, etc.	237,217,221

STOCKHOLDERS' EQUITY (the value of stockholders' interest in the corporation):

Preferred stock (at stated value of $100 a share)	283,564,400
Common Stock (at par value of $1⅔ per share)	479,159,142
Capital Surplus (principally what has been paid to the company for stock in addition to its par or stated value)	759,580,331
Net income retained for use in the business (earned surplus)	7,738,848,793
TOTAL STOCKHOLDERS' EQUITY	9,261,152,666
TOTAL LIABILITIES, RESERVES, AND STOCKHOLDERS' EQUITY	$13,273,082,524

has outstanding is listed first. Next is the data on common stocks, the number of shares that have been issued and their stated value at the time they were issued. This figure, in itself, is not meaningful for a person considering investing in the company. But the figure is of great importance when considered with those that follow. The stated value of the stock may be less than the company received when it sold its shares. The difference between what the company received for the shares and their stated value is the next item on the balance sheet. It is listed as capital surplus. This item is usually followed by another, retained earnings, or earned surplus. The figure tells how much of its earnings a company has kept, instead of paying everything it has made to shareowners as dividends.

By some simple arithmetic, you can figure the "book" value of a share of common stock from the figures given under stockholders' equity. Book value is often referred to in investment reports. To calculate it, you must sum up the figures given for the stated value of the common stock, the capital surplus, and retained earnings. Then subtract the stated value of the preferred stock, if there is any. Divide the result by the number of shares of common stock outstanding listed in the financial reports, and you get the book value of a share of the company's common stock.

Some investors give great consideration to the book value of a stock. If the book value is more than the market price, the stock may seem to be a bargain. Other investors, while not entirely neglecting book value, look to other factors to determine what they are willing to pay for a stock. A company's earnings are a better indication of the real value of its stock than its book value.

Earning statements are usually shorter than balance sheets and may consist of no more than a dozen or so lines. First is a figure telling how much the company took in from its normal business operations. The figure is usually listed as sales or operating revenues. There may be a second line with the words, other income. When you analyze an earning statement, it may be important to learn what the "other income" represents. If it comes from a source that will not continue to produce income (for instance, from the sale of one of the company's buildings), the item obviously should be disregarded in judging the future earning possibilities of the company.

After income, expenses are listed, the cost of operating the business, the cost of goods sold, taxes, and so on. One of the usual expense items is depreciation (how much of that $7,500 truck was used up during the year). The difference between income and expenses is stated as net earnings or net income.

At the bottom of earning statements, there is frequently a summary telling how much was earned on each share of common stock, how much was paid out as dividends, and how much of the earnings was retained in the business.

The deduction for depreciation on a company's earnings statement does not represent a cash outlay. It is a bookkeeping figure. It reflects the decrease in the value of fixed assets that were paid for in the past. Thus the cash that the company has taken in during the year may be greater than the net earnings shown on its earnings statement. Investors, therefore, consider "cash flow," which is net earnings plus depreciation. The figure is important because it tells how much the company has for the payment of dividends and for buying new and more efficient equipment. A company with a large cash flow is in a good position to keep up with technological improvements.

A study of the balance sheet and earnings statement of a corporation provides many clues to its business health. One is the relationship between current assets and current liabilities. Only if current assets are much greater (twice as much or more) than current liabilities has a company sufficient working capital to carry on its business successfully.

Another clue is the relationship between sales (or operating revenues) and profits, in other words, the margin of profit. A company's sales may increase, but if there is also a big jump in its expenses, the company may be in trouble. Margin of profit is figured by dividing the amount reported as profit by the amount reported for sales. The resulting percentage should be compared with the company's margin of profit in the past and with the profit records of other companies in the same line of business.

The most important test of a company's business health is how much it earns per share of common stock. Stockholders generally are concerned with earnings. The dividend paid on a share of stock is the portion of the company's earnings that a shareholder receives; the earn-

GENERAL MOTORS CORPORATION
STATEMENT OF CONSOLIDATED INCOME*
For the year ended December 31, 1967

In this statement the income of General Motors Corporation and of its subsidiary companies engaged in manufacturing and wholesale selling is lumped together. It is therefore called a consolidated statement. Income from other subsidiary companies (known as non-consolidated subsidiaries) is shown as a separate item.

NET SALES	$20,026,252,468
(General Motors Corporation and consolidated companies)	
Share of earnings of non-consolidated subsidiary companies (including General Motors Acceptance Corporation which finances automobile sales)	57,026,345
Other income (principally interest earned) less various deductions	56,324,960
TOTAL	20,139,603,773

LESS:

Cost of manufacturing products, selling, administrative expenses	16,306,583,932
Depreciation of buildings and equipment	712,643,765
Provision for Bonus Plan and Stock Option Plan for employees and executives	107,000,000
Provision for income taxes	1,386,100,000
TOTAL	18,512,327,697
NET INCOME for the year	1,627,276,076
Dividends on preferred stocks	12,928,276
AMOUNT EARNED ON COMMON STOCK	$ 1,614,347,800
Average number of shares of common stock outstanding during the year	285,341,822
AMOUNT EARNED PER SHARE OF COMMON STOCK	$5.66
NET INCOME RETAINED FOR USE IN THE BUSINESS (earned surplus) at beginning of the year	$ 7,208,856,342
NET INCOME for the year	1,627,276,076
TOTAL	8,836,132,418

DIVIDENDS PAID

Preferred stock	12,928,276
Common stock	1,084,355,349
TOTAL CASH DIVIDENDS	1,097,283,625
NET INCOME RETAINED FOR USE IN THE BUSINESS (earned surplus) at end of the year	$ 7,738,848,793

* This tabulation is a slightly revised version of the one included in the corporation's Annual Report issued in 1968.

ings per share (which in every flourishing company are more than the dividends) represent the shareholder's real return on his investment. The dividend is money he may spend; the balance of the earnings is money that the company is reinvesting for him. If it is wisely reinvested, it will produce greater dividends in the future.

Many investors decide how much they are willing to pay for a stock on the basis of its earnings per share, and that is why the price-earnings ratio of a stock is given in every investment analysis. To determine the price-earnings ratio, divide the market price of the stock by its earnings per share. If a stock is selling at $20 a share and the company reported earnings for the year of $1 per share, the price-earnings ratio for the stock is 20. The price-earnings ratio of any stock depends on its popularity and buyers' guesses as to its future. Some of the most popular stocks, sometimes called glamour issues, may sell at prices that are more than 60 times earnings. When a buyer pays such a high price for a stock, he is counting either on a sharp increase in earnings or on a further increase in its market price.

There is no certainty as to how market prices will move, but analyzing a company's balance sheets and earnings statements helps in making an intelligent guess as to a company's prospects.

10

INVESTING AS A
MEMBER OF A GROUP

At many schools the study of economics includes practical experience in investing. Students get their experience by joining their school's investors' club and buying stock.

One of the first of such investors' clubs was organized back in 1955 at the high school in Nyack, New York. The Skidoo Investment Fund, as the club is named, has been so successful that schools throughout the country have used it as a model.

Membership in the Skidoo Investment Fund is limited to students in the twelfth-grade economics course. Instead of paying dues, members buy shares in the Fund. A share costs 50¢, and no member may buy more than ten. In an average year the Fund's capital, obtained from the sale of its shares, averages $80–$90.

Before making any decision about what stock to buy, members of the Fund start, as do many intelligent investors, by choosing the industries in which to put their money. In one recent year the Fund chose electronics, clothing manufacturing, and paper goods as the fields with the most interesting investment possibilities. Electronics was chosen because of the rapid development of the industry, and clothing manufacturing because times were good, and during good times the sale of clothing increases. The choice of the paper industry was based on the fact that many of its products have only a one-time use. Wrapping paper, newspaper, milk cartons, napkins, towels, cups, etc., are discarded after being used once. The continuing need for new supplies provides paper goods manufacturers with a dependable source of income.

After the choice of industries has been made, members of the Skidoo Investment Fund decide on the particular companies in which to invest. The records of a number of companies in the selected industries are considered. Members of the Fund are designated to report on the companies' incomes, the relationship between income and expenses, the amount earned per share, and so on. The information is obtained from the companies' financial reports and from other published material, some of which is supplied by the Fund's broker. The broker, a resident of Nyack, takes a personal interest in the high school's investment club and assists it in many ways.

After a vote has been taken on the companies in which to buy stock, the broker fills the Fund's small order. Because persons under the age of twenty-one are legally prohibited from buying stock, the purchase is made in the name of the teacher of the economics course.

The Fund usually buys three shares of stock, one in each of the selected companies. Like many other investors, the students reduce their risk by following the old maxim, "Don't put all your eggs in one basket." If shares in only one company are bought and it fails to operate profitably, the investor ends up with a loss. However, if shares are bought in more than one company, a disappointing performance by one may be counterbalanced by the excellent performance of others. Reducing the risk by investing in companies operating in different fields is spoken of as diversification.

The Skidoo Investment Fund subscribes to the *Wall Street Journal,* and Fund members read the financial news regularly. Usually, they turn first to the tables giving the prices at which shares in their companies were sold on the previous day. Fund members keep a close watch on stock prices just as baseball fans do on batting averages.

One of the Fund's projects is charting the price changes of its stocks. The chart, prominently displayed in the room used for the economics course, gives a clear picture of price movements from week to week. Whether prices move up or down, the Skidoo Investment Fund does not sell its stocks until the end of the school term.

However, shares in the Fund may be sold at any time that owners wish to do so. The procedure is similar to the auction system used at stock markets. An owner who

wants to sell names his price, and Fund members who
want to buy say how much they are willing to pay. If the
market value of the stock owned by the Fund has increased (thereby making the Fund's shares worth more),
a member will ask more for his share than the 50¢ he
paid.

When the Skidoo Investment Fund sells its stock, the
money received, minus the broker's commission and
other costs involved in selling, is divided among members of the Fund according to the number of shares each
owns. If the stocks are sold for more than was paid for
them, Fund members make a profit on their investment;
if the market price of the stocks is down, members get
back less than they paid for their shares.

Some school investors' clubs do not sell their stocks
when the class completes its course. The investment club
of the Rapid City High School in South Dakota, for example, contributes its stocks to the school's scholarship
account.

Thousands of investors' clubs, which function similarly
to those in schools, have been established by groups of
adults. Members of such a group agree to pay a certain
amount into the club's treasury with which the club
makes investments. At one meeting members may vote to
purchase shares in an airline, at another in a food-proc-
essing company. The diversification of investments can
be quickly achieved by investors who pool their money.
This is one of the advantages of investing as a member of
a group.

Investors' clubs are true do-it-yourself organizations.

Members do the bookkeeping, deal with brokers, take care of correspondence and of all other details. To operate an investors' club successfully, members must devote a considerable amount of time to their club's affairs.

No work is involved when shares are bought in a professionally run investment company. The managers of such companies decide what securities to buy or to sell. Of course, shareholders pay for this service. After deductions for expenses, shareholders get the money earned by the company on its investments.

There are two types of investment companies: one is known as closed-end, the other as open-end. These terms take some explaining, but they really are very exact descriptions.

A closed-end investment company has a fixed number of shares. It may issue 50,000, 150,000, or any number that the organizers of the company decide upon when it is incorporated. Ordinarily, additional shares are not issued.

An open-end investment company, on the other hand, continuously issues shares—as many as people will buy. The more shares an open-end investment company sells, the more money it has to purchase securities. The most successful companies own securities with a market value of more than a billion dollars. Open-end companies are generally referred to as mutual funds.

Not only do closed-end investment companies and mutual funds have different policies as to the issuance of shares, but there is also a difference in the way their stock is bought and sold by investors. The stock of closed-

101

end investment companies is traded in exactly the same way as the stock of corporations engaged in other businesses. The stock may be bought or sold at stock markets (some of the largest closed-end investment companies are listed on the New York Stock Exchange) or in the over-the-counter market. The price of a share of stock is determined by bargaining between buyer and seller.

There is no free bargaining as to the price of stock in a mutual fund company. The company names the price. It is based on the mutual fund's net asset value. Net asset value is computed by totaling the market value of all the securities the fund owns and its uninvested cash and subtracting whatever sums the fund owes. The resultant figure, divided by the number of shares the company has outstanding, gives the asset value of a share. Thus, the value of a share in a mutual fund with net assets of $1,000,000 and 50,000 shares is $20.

Market prices of stocks continually change, and each change affects the asset value of a mutual fund's shares. If one of its shareowners wishes to sell, a mutual fund usually will pay him the price per share determined by its most recent computation and make no charge for the transaction. A unique feature of mutual funds is that they buy back their shares. There is no other way of selling them.

Naturally, the value of a share at any given time is the same whether a mutual fund is redeeming it or an investor is buying it. However, buyers are usually required to pay an additional fee for sales costs. In December, 1966, when the Securities and Exchange Commission com-

102

Mutual funds advertise their investment policy, but to obtain detailed information about a company, one must study its prospectus.

pleted its investigation of mutual funds, it stated that the typical charge for sales costs amounted to more than 9 percent. The Commission called such a charge unwarranted.

The Commission sharply criticized the sales charges made on the type of installment plan known as a "front-load contract." Under such a plan, a buyer contracts to invest a stated amount over a period of years, usually ten or twelve. But only about half of the amount he pays in during the first year may be applied to the purchase of shares. The other half goes to sales costs. Thus, if the investor cancels his installment contract at the end of one year, the shares he owns represent only about half the money he paid in. He ends up by losing about half of his investment. The SEC believes that front-load contracts should be prohibited by law and has submitted its recommendations to Congress.

Not all mutual funds make a selling charge. Shares in "no-load" companies are sold at their computed asset value. Companies that follow this policy usually include a statement about it in their advertisements and in the printed material given to prospective investors.

Since mutual funds continually issue new shares, they are bound by the provision in the securities law which requires that prospective buyers be given a printed booklet containing specified information about a company offering new stock. From such a booklet, called a prospectus, anyone considering investing in a mutual fund can find out about its financial record—its earnings, its investment policy, its sales charges, and so on. The printed facts are more important than what a salesman says. Salesmen may have a tendency to exaggerate.

The Investment Company Institute, the association of mutual funds, urges prospective investors to study a fund's investment policy before deciding to buy its shares. A mutual fund may state that it specializes in "growth" stocks, which means that when choosing securities, it is not as much concerned with the dividends they presently pay as with the possibility that the securities will increase in value. Another mutual fund may say that its emphasis is on securities currently paying dividends at a good rate. Some mutual funds invest only in common stocks; others balance their holdings by buying common stock, preferred stock, and bonds.

Not only should an investor contemplating the purchase of shares in a mutual fund study the investment programs of a number of companies so that he can determine which one most closely matches his own objectives, but he should also make a careful check of their financial records. Like companies operating in other fields, some mutual funds do better than others and pay their shareowners better dividends than others.

11

ATTENDING A
STOCKHOLDERS' MEETING

Once a year corporations hold a stockholders' meeting at which the president of the company reports on its record and prospects, and stockholders may pose questions and make proposals as to what they think should or should not be done. Until comparatively recently, most stockholders' meetings took place at the company's main office. This arrangement was satisfactory when many companies were owned by a comparatively small group of people who lived nearby the company.

Now many corporations are owned by such a large number of people that even though only a small percentage attend annual meetings, they cannot be accommodated at the company's headquarters. Therefore, it has become the practice for companies to rent a ballroom in a hotel and transform it into an auditorium, or to rent a theater for stockholders' meetings.

Another change is that meetings of many of the largest corporations are not always held in the vicinity of the company's head office. This change was recommended by stockholders. Since corporations are owned by people living throughout the country, the place where meetings are held is rotated. One year a company's annual meeting may be held in a city on the East Coast, the following year in a West Coast city, and the third year in a Midwest city. This gives more stockholders an opportunity to attend a meeting. Many people will make a trip of a hundred miles or so to be present at a meeting but would not consider attending if they had to travel thousands of miles.

Formerly, many stockholders' meetings were a combination of business and party. After the business session, elaborate refreshments were served. Some companies still give parties. In 1966 the Xerox Company, whose chief product is copying machines (you may have used one at a library to make a copy of a page of a book), rented a theater in Chicago for its annual shareowners' meeting. More than 1,600 shareowners, most of them from the Chicago area, attended the meeting and after it were served lunch. The company engaged a hotel to cater the luncheon. The food consumed included, among other items, 2,000 pounds of meat and 60 gallons of ice cream.

The luncheon bill paid by the company amounted to approximately $80,000. But the guests did not really get a free lunch. As owners of the company, it was their money that was used to pay the bill. All stockholders, those who attended and those who did not, indirectly paid for the party. Nowadays such parties are staged by comparatively few companies because shareowners objected to the expenditure of their money.

No two annual meetings are alike, but the general procedure is similar. The president of the company usually presides. Other officers and candidates for election to the board of directors are seated on the platform. After the meeting is called to order, the president introduces the men on the platform. He then makes a speech in which he summarizes the company's operations during the preceding year and its future plans. Much of the information is contained in the company's printed annual report, which is mailed to stockholders before the meeting. The real news announced at many meetings is how much the company earned during the first three months of the current year.

Much time may be spent debating the matters to be decided by stockholders' votes. In addition to the election of directors, such questions as whether their company should raise funds by the issuance of additional stock and whether the company should merge with another company, and so on may be up for voting.

If only the shareowners present at an annual meeting could exercise the right to vote, the vote would not be representative. Therefore, a system for absentee voting is used. When stockholders are notified of the date and place of the annual meeting, they are sent a statement concerning the proposals to be voted on and a ballot. Stockholders mark the ballot to indicate whether they are for or against the various proposals, and authorize persons named on the ballot (usually officers of the company) to vote for them. A written authorization by a shareholder to someone else to vote for him is known as a proxy. Because such an authorization is included on shareowners' ballots, they are generally called proxies.

The officers and directors of a company are in a strong position to win support for their proposals. However, shareowners may campaign to defeat a company's proposals and its candidates for the board of directors or to effect a change of policy. Such a campaign is usually spoken of as a "proxy fight." It is a fight to obtain stockholders' votes.

In most instances a proxy fight is spearheaded by the owner of a large number of shares. One recent proxy fight was led by a man who owned 10 percent of the stock of the moving picture producer, Metro-Goldwyn-Mayer. To defeat the plan proposed by the film company, he needed to convince holders of 41 percent of its stock to vote with him. He would then have the minimum required majority of 51 percent.

The stockholder conducted his campaign by mail, phone, and personal interviews. A stockholder who wishes to solicit the votes of his fellow owners can obtain a list of their names, addresses, and the number of shares they hold.

A proxy fight is costly for the stockholder who wages it and also for the company. Ordinarily, a company merely sends out ballots and does nothing more to induce share-owners to vote. But during a proxy fight, a company actively seeks its shareowners' votes. Sometimes it employs an organization that specializes in rounding up votes.

The MGM proxy fight was won by the company. The final votes were cast at a special meeting called by the company at which its president and the shareowner who disapproved of the company's proposals presented their arguments. The meeting lasted four hours and twenty-five minutes. It was held in a large New York City movie theater owned by MGM. Nearly every seat in the orchestra of the theater was occupied.

Unlike the rule governing most elections, that once a vote is cast it is final, stockholders have the privilege of changing their minds. A stockholder who has signed a proxy authorizing his vote to be cast for or against a plan may sign a new proxy before the meeting or a ballot at the meeting. The one with the latest date is the one that is counted. An announcement is usually made at stockholders' meetings that votes may be changed by marking another ballot.

At all meetings there is a period during which share-owners have an opportunity to ask questions, criticize, and suggest what they think the management should do. The question and answer period is usually the liveliest part of the meeting.

Often more than one person rises at about the same moment to request permission to speak. The presiding officer motions to the person whom he saw rise first, and then, in turn, other stockholders have a chance to speak.

Annual Meeting of Shareholders
Wednesday, April 17, 1968 • 2:00 P.M.
War Memorial Auditorium, Boston, Massachusetts

ADMITTANCE CARD
If you plan to attend—please check here ☐, fill in and return this form, *with your proxy*, in the enclosed envelope. A card of admission will be mailed to you.

REPORT OF MEETING
A brief report of the meeting will be sent with your July 1 dividend. If you wish to receive a more complete summary, similar to those of previous years, please check here ☐, fill in and return this form.

Please sign and return your proxy promptly whether you plan to attend the meeting or not. If you do attend, you may vote in person if you wish. Your vote is important regardless of the number of shares you own.

NAME _____
PLEASE PRINT

STREET _____
PLEASE PRINT

CITY _____

STATE _____ ZIP _____

Please do NOT return this form unless you plan to attend in person OR you wish to receive the longer report of the meeting.

American Telephone and Telegraph Company
195 Broadway, New York, N.Y. 10007

The booklet, sent with the notice of the annual meeting and the proxy, contained short biographies of the candidates for the board of directors. It also contained a shareholder's proposal that on most matters voting be by secret ballot. The directors recommended a vote against the proposal and gave their reasons. The proposal was defeated.

When the meeting room is large, all speakers use a microphone. Portable microphones are supplied by ushers stationed in strategic places in the room. Stockholders introduce themselves by giving their names and the number of shares they hold.

At one stockholders' meeting, a speaker who stated that he owned twelve shares of the company's stock argued for the approval of his proposal that the corporate officers who served on the board of directors should not be paid extra for attending meetings of the board. The regular fee was $100 a meeting. The proposal had been sent to the company months before the annual meeting and had been included in the material mailed to shareowners. The company had recommended that stockholders vote against it. At the meeting the sponsor of the proposal read it and then said:

"The officers of our company get good salaries, and I do not believe that they are entitled to an additional payment for serving as directors."

The president of the company disagreed, saying that directors have additional responsibilities and duties for which they are entitled to compensation.

The next to voice disapproval of the resolution was a man who announced that he owned 807 shares in the company. "That's nearly 70 times as many shares," he said, "as the man who is proposing eliminating payments to directors."

The president interrupted. "Every shareowner, whether he owns one share or a thousand, has a right to make proposals," he declared. The audience applauded.

The most important business at most stockholders' meetings is the election of a board of directors. Stockholders' real control of a corporation is through their right to elect the directors who designate the officers and set the policy for the company.

Ordinarily, members of a board of directors serve for one year, but they may be elected for many terms. In addition to officers of the company and one or more of its major stockholders, a board of directors usually includes lawyers, bankers, and other men prominent in various fields. The candidates' names, profession, or business and the number of shares they own in the company are listed in the printed material sent to shareowners with the proxies. The candidates usually attend the annual meeting of shareowners and, after being introduced, must be prepared to answer questions. The questions may be embarrassing.

For example, at the meeting of a large chain of food stores, a woman asked one candidate, a white-haired lawyer, whether he knew enough about the company's business to be an efficient director.

The lawyer replied that he believed he was qualified.

"I think your wife would be better qualified," the stockholder said. "Most of this company's customers are women, and I think it's about time we had a woman on our board of directors."

Most shareowners who speak at meetings do "homework" in advance. They come with prepared notes as to the points they wish to make and the questions they wish to ask. Many of the questions are about financial matters and are based on the figures in the balance sheet and earning statement printed in the company's annual report.

At one meeting a stockholder queried why the company's new factory was listed as costing $3,000,000 in-

113

stead of $2,500,000, which stockholders had previously been told would be the price.

The president replied that the additional expenditure had resulted from a modification of the original plan. He discussed in detail the reasons for modifying the plan. He said that as a result of the changes, the productive capacity of the factory had been greatly increased. Just as the president was finishing his explanation, a man seated in the front of the room requested permission to speak.

"I visited the factory during my vacation," he said. "The $3,000,000 it cost didn't seem excessive to me. I think anyone who makes a tour of the plant will feel the same way."

The stockholder was applauded, and the president said, "I wish all of you would inspect the plant. You own it and you should see it."

After a few more comments by stockholders, the Inspectors of Election assigned to count the votes reported to the president that the tabulations had been completed and handed him a sheet with the results. Soon after they were announced, the meeting was adjourned. Many large companies send all stockholders a printed report of their annual meeting. All the highlights of the meeting are included.

12

HOW TO READ
THE MARKET NEWS

In early evening news broadcasts and telecasts, brief reports about the trading at stock markets are frequently
included. The announcer states the prices at which
shares in a selected list of companies were sold and, in
addition, gives a general round-up of market news—
whether trading was active or light, whether the general
price movement was up or down, etc.

Such summaries give the highlights. For the details
people depend on newspapers. If their local paper does
not supply as much information as they desire, they subscribe to an out-of-town paper that does. The *Wall Street
Journal*, which specializes in news of the financial world,
has readers from coast to coast.

Many city newspapers publish a business and financial

section containing tabulations of stock exchange transactions and articles about the earnings reported by companies, new bond issues, decisions of the Securities and Exchange Commission, negotiations being conducted for the purchase of one company by another, and so on. The advertisements include insertions by brokerage firms, mutual-fund companies, put and call dealers, announcements by investment brokers of new stock and bond issues they are offering, and sometimes notices by bond issuers that they have called in certain bonds for redemption.

The news of greatest interest to most people is in the tabulations of stock market transactions. At first glance the tabulations look formidable. They are printed in small type, and the lines are close together. This typographical arrangement is used to conserve space. Each security listed has a line for itself. And there are many thousands of securities. A day's tabulation of New York Stock Exchange transactions fills about a page and a half, and those of the American Stock Exchange about two-thirds of a page. The over-the-counter quotations supplied by the National Association of Security Dealers fill a page. In addition to these long tabulations, there are shorter ones listing the sales at the country's smaller stock markets. Few people read the tabulations straight through. They look up the particular securities in which they are interested.

Stocks and bonds are listed by the names of the companies that issued them. The names are given in alphabetical order, but they are abbreviated and sometimes

116

are difficult to recognize. Can Dry for Canada Dry is one of the most obvious of the abbreviations. The full name of a company provides a clue to its abbreviation and also to its alphabetical position in a tabulation.

Most newspapers get stock and bond tables either from the Associated Press or the United Press. Both of these news services prepare the data in similar form. A full tabulation consists of nine columns. Some newspapers may omit certain columns or listings, but about 140 newspapers print the complete list of New York Stock Exchange transactions.

In a complete tabulation of the stocks traded, the first column on the left is headed High, and the one next to it Low. These columns provide historical background. The figures listed are the highest and lowest prices paid for a share of the stock during the year.

The third column is headed Stocks and Div. (dividends) in Dollars. This is the column in which you look for the abbreviated name of the company in whose securities you are interested. If a company has issued both preferred and common stock, the preferred is identified by the letters, pf, after the company's name. The figures that follow tell the amount of the dividend payable on the preferred stock. When a company has more than one class of preferred stock, each is listed on a separate line with its yearly dividend. Since dividend payments on preferred stock are fixed, the rate payable identifies a particular issue. The dividend figures listed for common stocks are estimates based on the last payments made.

After some of the dividend figures, there is a letter. Its

117

meaning is given in the footnotes to the tabulation. Reading the footnotes is important. For example, the letter a, after the dividend figure, indicates that the company has made one or more extra dividend payments to shareowners. The letter x is a warning that anyone who buys the stock will not be eligible for a dividend payment soon to be paid. X stands for ex-dividend, that is, without dividend.

For bookkeeping purposes it is necessary for companies to limit dividend payments to shareowners whose names are in its stock register on a specified date. Assume that the board of directors of Typical Company has voted a 50¢ per share dividend payable on May 26. In announcing the dividend, the company states that the payment will be made to shareowners "of record" on May 5. The three weeks between the cutoff and the payment dates are needed by Typical Company to prepare and mail its dividend checks.

Although the cutoff date is May 5, x is printed in the May 2 newspaper tabulation of market transactions. No mistake has been made about the date. The New York Stock Exchange, where Typical's stock is traded, allows four business days for the delivery of stock and the transferring of stock certificates. For a buyer to get his name in Typical Company's records by May 5, he would have to purchase its stock on May 1 at the latest. Shareowners who sell after that date are entitled to Typical's dividend payments.

Whether there was much or little trading in a company's stock is learned from the fourth column in the tabulation of market transactions. The column is headed

New York Stock Exchange Transactions

| 1968 High. Low. | Stocks and Div. In Dollars. | Sls. 100s. | First. | High. | Low. | Net Last. Chge. |

A—B—C—D

1968 High.	Low.	Stocks and Div. In Dollars.	Sls. 100s.	First.	High.	Low.	Last.	Net Chge.
55¾	47⅞	Abbott Lab 1	48	55⅜	55⅜	54¼	54⅞	— ¼
34¾	28	Abex Cp 1.60	19	33⅛	33¾	33	33¾	+ ⅜
48	39½	ACF Ind 2.20	38	47½	47½	47	47½	+ ½
41¾	36	Acme Mkt 2b	14	40¼	40⅜	40⅛	40⅛	— ⅜
17⅝	16	Adams Exp	16	17¼	17¼	17	17⅛	.....
29½	22⅝	Ad Millis .20	139	25⅞	26½	25½	26⅜	+ ⅞
80½	52	Address 1.40	148	72⅛	72⅛	70½	70½	—1⅞
25⅛	16½	Admiral	195	20½	22	20½	21¾	+1½
64	47¼	Aeroquip 1b	22	62	62⅞	61¾	61⅞	+ ¾
41⅝	32⅝	Air Prod .20b	23	33	33	32⅞	32⅞	— ⅛
123½	106	Air Pd pf4.75	1	106	106	106	106	—1½
36⅞	28½	AirRedtn 1.50	65	30	30	29¾	29⅞	— ¼
12⅝	8⅛	AJ Industries	476	10¾	11⅜	10¾	10⅞	+ ⅛
19½	17⅜	Ala Gas .96	2	18⅛	18¼	18⅛	18¼	+ ⅛
43⅞	32	Alberto C .20	19	40⅛	40⅜	39⅝	40	— ⅜
27⅜	22	AlcanAlum 1	211	22¾	22⅞	22⅜	22¾	— ⅛
17⅞	12¼	Alleg Cp .10e	70	14⅜	14⅜	14	14	— ¼
65	45	Alleg 6pf .60	3	50	50	50	50	.....
72¾	60⅛	AllegLud 2.40	26	64	65¾	64	65¾	+2⅛
76⅜	67	AllegLud pf 3	5	68	69	68	69	+1½
24¼	20⅝	Alleg Pw 1.20	130	22¾	22¾	22⅛	22⅛	— ½
31⅞	24¾	AllenInd 1.40	5	30⅝	30⅝	30½	30½	.....
43	34	AlliedCh 1.90	130	36½	36¾	36¼	36⅝	+ ⅛
33¼	24½	Allied Kid 1	14	29⅜	29⅜	29⅛	29⅛	.....
49	44¼	Allied Mills 2	2	49	49	49	49	.....
63¾	37¾	Allied Pd .60	18	52½	52½	51¾	51⅞	— ⅝
51¼	35⅝	Allied Str 1.40	41	50	50	49	49	—1
22	16	AlliedSup .60	77	16⅞	16⅞	16⅝	16⅝	— ⅛
38⅛	28⅜	Allis Chal 1	428	32⅞	33⅛	32½	32¾	+ ¾
16¾	12	Alpha P Cem	72	16½	16⅞	16¾	16⅞	+ ¾
14¾	10⅝	Alside .20	69	14¾	15	14⅜	14⅜	— ⅛
81½	65½	Alcoa 1.80	80	70⅜	70½	70	70¼	.....
64	41⅝	AMBAC .60	45	60	60	59	59½	— ⅝
43	28½	Amerace 1.20	14	41	41⅛	40½	40¾	— ¼
87⅝	75	Amerada 3	143	86	86¼	84¾	84¾	—1¾
38½	31	AAirFiltr .80	15	33⅞	34	33⅜	34	— ⅛
33⅞	24	Am Airlin .80	733	25¼	25⅝	24⅞	24⅞	— ⅝
28	21	Am Baker 1	27	26⅞	26⅞	26⅝	26⅞	+ ⅜
69	43¾	AmBdcst 1.60	100	56⅞	57⅝	56	56½	— ¼
		Cän 2.20		51¾	52½	51½	52¼	...
		1.7				30¼	30	30¼

Newspapers that print a full tabulation of transactions at the New York Stock Exchange devote about a page and a half to the listings. In the section shown above, the most active trading was in American Airlines stock. During the day 73,300 shares were traded. The price fell five-eighths of a point or $.625 per share.

SLS 100s. SLS is the abbreviation for sales, and 100s means that the figures listed are to be multiplied by 100.

The next columns, First, High, Low, Last, tell the first price paid for the stock on the day covered by the tabulation, the highest and lowest prices that were paid that day, and the price of the last sale. The dollar sign is omitted, and fractions are used for parts of a dollar.

The last column, Net Chge. (Change) gives the increase or decrease between the closing price of the day covered and the closing price of the preceding day. A plus sign indicates that the price increased, a minus sign that the closing price was below that of the preceding day.

The tabulations of bond transactions at exchanges are similar to those of stocks. The bond tables, however, are short because comparatively few bonds are traded at organized exchanges. Most are sold over-the-counter.

In reporting the prices of bonds sold at exchanges, the last digit is omitted. Thus, a price of 99 means that the sale was made at $990, which, for a bond with a face value of $1,000, would be at a discount of $10. When the price includes a fraction, it means a fraction of 100. A price listed as 94⅝ is $946.25.

Stock or bond tabulations must be read over a period of time to draw conclusions from them. The figures for a single day, or even for a week, do not provide an adequate basis for forming a judgment. And in order to decide whether the stock of any one company is doing well or badly, you must know the market's record as a whole. If the general price movement is up, it is normal for the price of the stock that you are following to go up. Or if generally prices are falling, it is normal for the market value of a particular stock to be down.

Information about general market conditions is prepared by experts, and the results of their computations are known as averages or indexes. There are many of them, but the one most widely publicized is the Dow Jones Average. It was started in 1896 by Charles Dow, founder of the *Wall Street Journal.*

Dow Jones today publishes four averages, one for industrial companies, a second for railroads, and a third for utility companies—the companies that supply gas and electric current. The fourth average is a combination of the other three. The Dow Jones industrial average, the one most frequently quoted, is based on 30 selected stocks. Many are of the type known as "blue chips." They are stocks of well-known companies that have a long history of financial success. The Dow Jones industrial list includes General Motors, American Telephone and Telegraph Company, and General Electric. The 30 stocks used to compute the Dow Jones industrial average account for about one-third of the market value of all the common stocks sold at the New York Stock Exchange.

If you want to determine the average price of three stocks with a market value of $30, $20, and $10, you would total the prices, divide by three, and get an average price of $20.

The average price for any number of stocks is figured in exactly the same way. But since averages are computed over a period of time, a number of mathematical adjustments must be made if the average for one year is to be at all comparable with the average for preceding years. Not only are substitutions occasionally made in the companies included in the average, but companies also split their stocks, issuing two shares for one, three for one, and so on.

There are various methods for adjusting averages for stock splits. The Dow Jones method is to adjust its divisor. Each time there is a stock split, the divisor is reduced. Originally, the divisor used for its average of 30 industrial stocks was 30; by 1967 the divisor was 2.245.

Averages are important only as an indication of price movements. If the Dow Jones industrial average goes up from 900 to 909, it means that the market prices of stocks in industrial companies, as reflected by the average, have increased by 1 percent. It does not mean that the stocks are selling for anything like $909.

The index prepared by Standard & Poor's is based on the price of 500 stocks sold at the New York Stock Exchange. In 1966 the New York Stock Exchange began to issue its own index based on the price of all common stocks listed on the Exchange. It is probably the most realistic index of stock prices. But the Dow Jones industrial average is still the one most frequently quoted.

Today more people are following business and financial news than ever before. The increased interest is partly due to the tremendous growth in the number of people who own stocks and bonds. A person who has a financial stake in a company naturally is interested in news about it and in the market value of his investment.

But many people who own no securities also are concerned with what is happening in the business world. They know that it affects them either directly or indirectly.

If a company reports increased earnings, its stockholders look forward to the possibility of bigger dividends and to an appreciation in the value of their stock. The same earnings report encourages people who work for the company to anticipate the continuance of full-time employment and the possibility of higher wages.

The effect of a large company's record of earnings extends beyond its shareowners and employees. After a good year the company may increase production, purchase more machines, and erect new buildings, thus giving employment to many. A large percentage of the company's increased earnings will be paid out in dividends and wages. The money the company pays out will be respent for a great variety of things that people want—homes, automobiles, vacations—and these expenditures will lead to more employment, more profit for other companies, and then to more buying. The buying cycle spreads in an ever widening circle. The fact is that the success or failure of our big publicly owned corporations determines the economic condition of the nation.

INDEX

Illustrations are indicated by italicized numbers.